EGYPTIAN
MYTHOLOGY

EGYPTIAN MYTHOLOGY

MYTHS AND LEGENDS OF EGYPT, PERSIA, ASIA MINOR, SUMER AND BABYLON

RACHEL STORM

SELECT
EDITIONS

Select Editions imprint specially produced for Selectabook Ltd

Produced by Anness Publishing Limited, Hermes House,88-89 Blackfriars Road
London
SE1 8HA
tel. 020 7401 2077
fax 020 7633 9499

Publisher: Joanna Lorenz
Managing Editor: Helen Sudell
Project Editor: Emma Gray
Contributing Editor: Beverley Jollands
Editorial Assistant: Helen Marsh
Designer: Mario Bettella, Artmedia
Map Illustrator: Stephen Sweet
Picture Researcher: Adrian Bentley
Editorial Reader: Richard McGinlay
Production: Don Campaniello

Previously published as part of a larger compendium, *The Encyclopedia of Eastern Mythology*

1 3 5 7 9 10 8 6 4 2

Page 1: Isis, sister of Osiris.
Page 2: The mask of Tutankhamen.
Page 3: Ishtar, the goddess of love and war.
Page 4: Ramases II in battle.
Page 5: The weighing of the soul, part of the Egyptian journey to the underworld.

Publisher's Note
The entries in this book are all listed alphabetically. Where more than one name exists for a character the entry is listed under the name used in the original country of origin for that particular myth. Names in italic capital letters indicate that that name has an individual entry. Special feature spreads examine specific mythological themes in more detail. If a character is included in a special feature spread it is noted at the end of their individual entry.

CONTENTS

INTRODUCTION

T HE ANCIENT MIDDLE EAST, the so-called "cradle of civilization", was the birthplace of Judaism, Islam and Christianity, the three faiths that came to have such an immense impact on human culture and, by tradition, originated amongst the descendants of Shem, one of the sons of Noah. Zoroastrianism, probably the most powerful religion of its time, also arose in the Middle East, whereas the wider area of West Asia witnessed the rise of the powerful Egyptian and Hittite empires.

What was it about this region that enabled it to bear witness to such remarkable achievements? One answer at least lies in the geography of the area: it was here that crop farming first began, and with it the beginnings of a settled, civilized way of life, which proceeded to bear rich cultural fruits.

The annual flooding of the Nile inspired many of the myths of ancient Egypt. The people there depended on the revival of the parched land for their livelihood, a concern that was reflected in the myth of Osiris, their dying-and-rising vegetation god, who finally retired from life to rule over the underworld. A preoccupation with death haunts Egyptian mythology, prompted by this sense of man's vulnerability in the face of forces beyond his control. Even the great sun god, Ra, was believed to die each evening and be born again at dawn.

It was on the fertile land produced by the Nile's annual floodings that Egypt's first city states grew up, each with its own gods. Eventually, around 3100 BC, these separate states were unified under a succession of pharaohs. Many of the local gods were admitted into the national pantheon, giving

SYMBOLIZING the divine relationship between pharaohs and the gods, Horemheb, the last Egyptian pharaoh of the 18th dynasty, sits beside the god Horus, son of Isis and Osiris. (C. 1320 BC.)

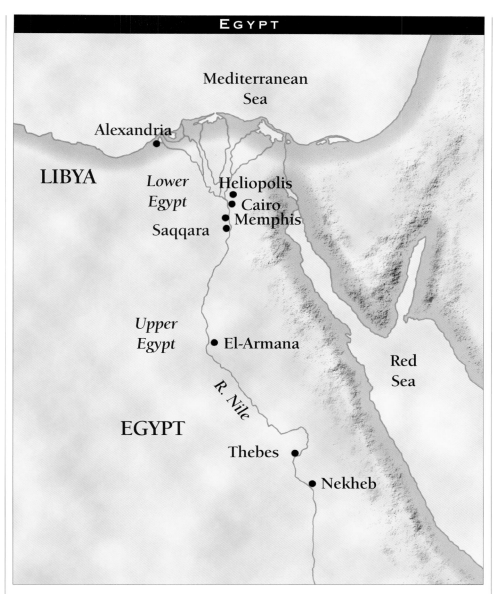

EGYPT

Mediterranean
Sea

Alexandria

LIBYA

Lower Egypt   Heliopolis
                Cairo
                Memphis
Saqqara

Upper Egypt   El-Armana

                Red
                Sea

EGYPT   R. Nile

        Thebes

            Nekheb

featured dying and rising gods. The Mesopotamians' existence was, however, much more precarious than that of the Egyptians. Not only could the flooding of their rivers be sudden and unpredictable, but the people were also under constant threat from marauding tribes and foreign invaders. Their myths, therefore, tended to portray life as a constant battle against the forces of chaos.

Despite its political instability, ancient Mesopotamia produced an extensive written literature. As a result, the Mesopotamian deities and myths were transmitted to other West Asian peoples, including the Assyrians and Hittites. The Hittites, who originally hailed from Anatolia, came to be known in the Old Testament as one of the peoples occupying Canaan, the promised land of the Israelites. Many of the ancestors of the Israelites had themselves migrated from Mesopotamia to Canaan soon after 2000 BC; some of them continued into Egypt where, at a date which is uncertain, they were taken into slavery by a pharaoh. However, in the

BAAL, an ancient fertility god, is a dying and rising god whose actions symbolized the growth and decay of vegetation. (BRONZE AGE, 1400–1300 BC.)

rise to a vast and splendid array of deities who flourished virtually unopposed by alien beliefs. Seen as divinely appointed mediators between the world of men and the gods, the pharaohs gave a political and religious focus to Egyptian civilization and culture. Their power was such that it came to extend into Canaan and Syria. However, in about 1387 BC the pharaoh Akhenaten instigated vast religious reforms, which, though eventually overturned when he died, began to weaken Egyptian power.

Like the Egyptians, the Mesopotamian settlers were attracted to the rich land left by the flooding of rivers. The Sumerians, a non-Semitic people (not descended from Shem), had settled in Mesopotamia, the area lying between the rivers Tigris and Euphrates, around 4000 BC. Some 2,000 years later, Babylon was made the region's capital and Sumer was gradually absorbed into Babylonia. The livelihood of these Mesopotamians, like that of the Egyptians, depended on the agricultural cycle, and their pantheon likewise

MOSES delivered the tribes of Israel from slavery in Egypt and led them through the desert to freedom. Here he strikes the rock to produce water. (19TH CENTURY ENGRAVING.)

13th century BC, Moses led the Israelites out of slavery in Egypt and back towards Canaan. On this journey, they made a solemn promise to worship only one god – Yahweh.

The Canaanite pantheon, which the Israelites encountered at the end of their journey, was dominated by the god of rain, fertility and storms, Baal. Many other gods also went under this name, which translates as "Lord", but the chief Baal was a warlike dying and rising god. His attributes reflected the Canaanite way of life which, like that of all the other peoples of the region, was closely bound up with the agricultural cycle.

As the tribes settled in Canaan, they united in their worship of Yahweh, who became the supreme god, although rites associated with

ZOROASTER, the great religious reformer of ancient Iran, receives fire and the law of reform, which is brought to him by Ahura Mazda, the principle of good. At the age of 30, Zoroaster received numerous revelations from the Amesa Spentas, or holy immortals. (19TH CENTURY ILLUSTRATION.)

other gods persisted for some time. The followers of the new faith were based around Jerusalem. In 587 BC, the city was conquered by the Babylonians, and the leading Israelites were taken into exile in Babylon. Nearly 50 years later, the Achaemenids of Iran, whom the Greeks called Persians, conquered Babylon in turn.

The Persian conquerors introduced the Babylonians to their Zoroastrian faith, which, though often loosely adhered to, saw the world as in the grip of the forces of good and evil. Zoroaster, who founded the religion and who is now believed to have lived around 1200 BC, had preached of his vision of a single, supreme god. Faced with encroaching monotheism, and sometimes directly overthrown, the Mesopotamian gods finally began to lose their power. In 525 BC the Persians also occupied Egypt. Since the pharaoh Akhenaten had tried to bring about religious reform back in 1367 BC, the country had never quite recovered its harmony or strength, and its glorious pantheon of gods was becoming increasingly threatened by outside beliefs.

Monotheism, as preached by both the Israelites and the Zoroastrians, was thus beginning to threaten the vast and dramatic array of gods and goddesses until then prevalent across West Asia, and the region was to see yet more turmoil. Over the following centuries it was overrun by the Greeks and Romans. However, Cybele, the great mother goddess of Asia Minor, Isis, the great mother goddess of Egypt, and Mithra, originally an ancient Iranian sun god, all arrived in Rome. There they became the focus of mystery cults, which flourished in the early centuries of the Christian era. When many of the old gods of West Asia were losing their power, these ancient deities were believed to renew the spirit and put their devotees in touch with the divine.

Monotheism eventually triumphed in West Asia. By the time the prophet Muhammad was born, around AD 570, Judaism and later Christianity had already spread throughout the region, and had also encroached on the Arabian peninsula. With the arrival of the strictly monotheistic Islam, the days of the old gods were numbered.

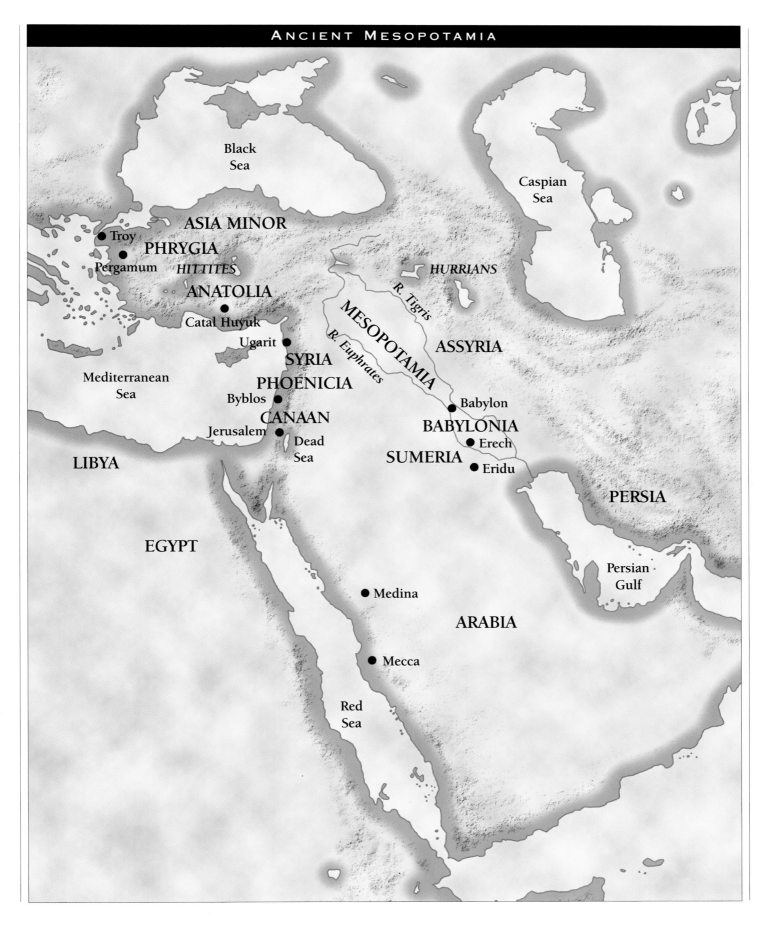

ANCIENT MESOPOTAMIA

Black Sea

Caspian Sea

ASIA MINOR

• Troy
PHRYGIA
Pergamum
HITTITES

HURRIANS

ANATOLIA
•
Catal Huyuk

R. Tigris

MESOPOTAMIA

R. Euphrates

ASSYRIA

Ugarit •

SYRIA

PHOENICIA

Mediterranean Sea

Byblos •

CANAAN

Babylon •

Jerusalem •

• Dead Sea

BABYLONIA

SUMERIA

• Erech

LIBYA

• Eridu

PERSIA

EGYPT

Persian Gulf

• Medina

ARABIA

• Mecca

Red Sea

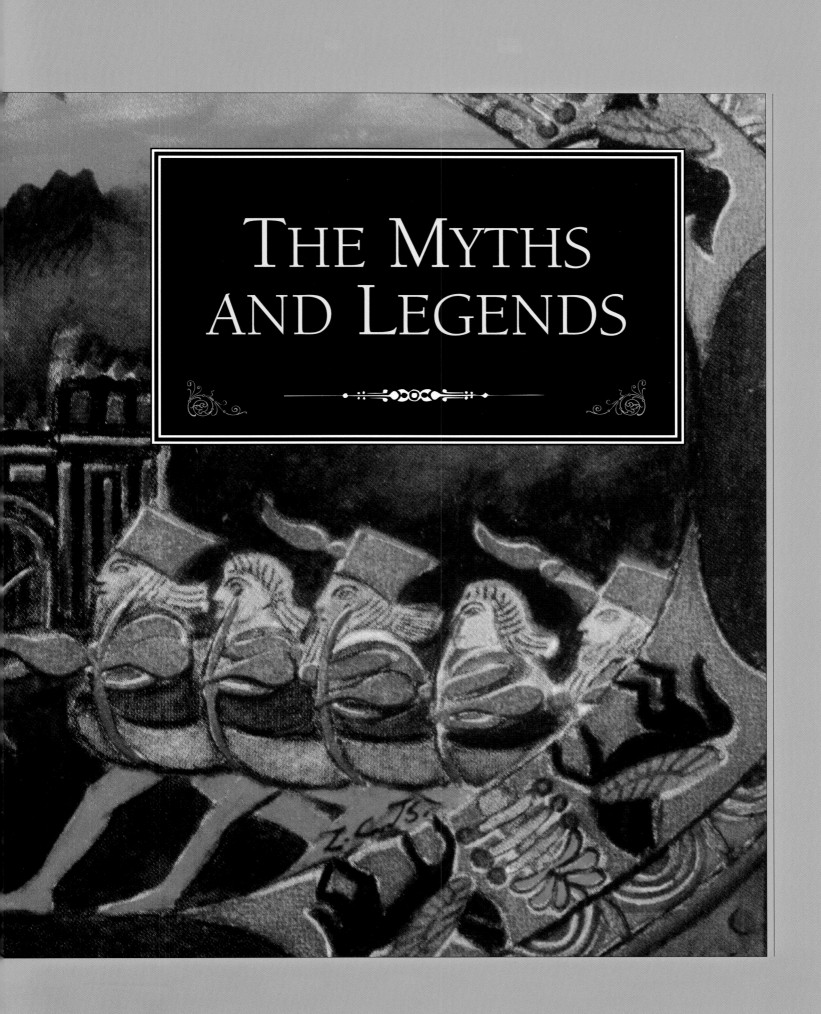

THE MYTHS AND LEGENDS

A

ABRAHAM, whose name means "Father of a Multitude", is a major character in the Old Testament, and is referred to in the earliest sources simply as "the Hebrew". The founder of the Hebrew people, he was the first patriarch, the husband of Sarah and the father of Isaac. He lived around 2000–1800 BC and was a devout believer of and subservient to God, representing an ideal for Hebrews to emulate. In Islam, Abraham, or Ibrahim, is known as the "Friend of God". He is regarded as the propagator of the original pure monotheism, the "religion of Abraham", which was restored and perfected by the Prophet Muhammad. Abraham is also said to have rebuilt the KA'ABA, the sacred shrine at Mecca, after it had been destroyed by the flood.

ABRAHAM (below), the father of the Israelite tribes, prepares to sacrifice his son, Isaac. (STAINED GLASS, ENGLAND.)

ABRAHAM (above) is known in Islam as Ibrahim, the "Friend of God". His son, Isaac, bears wood for the fire on which he is to be sacrificed. (19TH CENTURY ENGRAVING.)

ABZU see *APSU*.

ADAD was the Akkadian-Babylonian god of the wind, rain and thunder. He was usually said to be the son of *ANU*, and he was one of the deities who inflicted a deluge on humanity. However, he also brought helpful winds and rain and caused the annual flooding of the rivers, thereby bringing fertility to the land. As a result, Adad was often referred to as "Lord of Abundance". He could also see into the future. Adad was often represented standing on a bull and holding thunderbolts or lightning flashes in each hand.

ADAD (right), stands on the back of a bull, holding a bundle of thunderbolts in his hand. He is the Akkadian-Babylonian god of wind and rain. (NEO-ASSYRIAN BASALT RELIEF ON A STELE, 8TH CENTURY BC.)

ADAM, according to the Old Testament story, was the first man. God made him from dust and gave him a beautiful garden in which to live. Everything in the garden belonged to Adam, except for the fruit of one tree. Together with his consort *EVE*, Adam ate the forbidden fruit. As a result, the couple immediately lost their innocence and incurred the wrath of God. They were thrown out of the garden and had to work to survive.

According to the Jewish mystical system known as the Kabbalah, Adam both symbolized and embraced cosmic perfection. With Adam's fall, the material world was created and the light of his divine nature was broken up into countless minute sparks. These sparks are the lights that illuminate human souls. At the end of time, they will be reunited into perfection once more. (See also *SERPENTS AND DRAGONS*)

ADAPA, a wise man of Babylonian mythology, was created by the great god *EA* in order to be his priest in the holy city of Eridu and to rule over the people. Ea gave Adapa numerous good qualities, including wisdom and prudence, but did not make him immortal. Adapa spent much of his time fishing in the waters of the Persian Gulf.

One day, the south wind blew so strongly that it overturned his boat, sending him plunging into the depths. Adapa was furious and cursed the wind, causing it to cease blowing. Hearing what had happened, the supreme god *ANU* grew troubled that a mere mortal should have so much power. He summoned Adapa to his court and planned to send him to the land of the dead by giving him the food of death.

Ea, however, heard of Anu's plot and warned Adapa to accept no food or drink from the supreme god. Ea also told Adapa how to placate both Anu and the deities who lived with him. Adapa followed

ADAM and EVE were tempted by the serpent to eat the forbidden fruit. God banished them from the garden, and they had to work. (SPANISH SCHOOL, 12TH CENTURY.)

Ea's advice so punctiliously that Anu, rather than offering the food of death, offered him the food of life. However, Adapa remembered Ea's warning and refused the food, thereby losing his chance of becoming immortal.

Adapa, who was also credited with having invented speech, laid the foundations of civilized life.

ADONIS was a Phoenician deity who was later assimilated into the Greek pantheon. His name comes from the Semitic word *adoni*, meaning "My Lord, My Master". His worship was prevalent throughout Phoenicia, but it was most fervent in the city of Byblos, where his greatest temple stood.

Adonis symbolizes vegetation scorched by the heat of the summer sunshine. According to Greek legend, he was born from a myrtle or myrrh tree. His mother, Myrrha, had been changed into the tree by the gods who had sought to protect her from the wrath of her father, the king. Unbeknown to the king, Myrrha had seduced him and had conceived a child. Soon after Adonis was born, Aphrodite, the goddess of love, discovered the

young deity. She hid him in a chest which she gave for safekeeping to Persephone, the goddess of the underworld. However, Persephone opened the chest and was so struck with the beauty of the child that she decided to keep him. Aphrodite appealed to Zeus, who decided that Adonis should spend a third of each year with himself, a third with Persephone and a third with the goddess of love.

When Adonis grew up, Aphrodite fell passionately in love with him. Out hunting one day, the god was killed by a boar. It is at this point, in some versions of the myth, that Aphrodite, mad with grief, managed to secure his release from the underworld for half of each year. In Byblos, it was said that he returned from the dead when the river ran red with soil brought down from the hills by rain.

The Adonia, the annual festivals that commemorated the god's death, were beautiful and opulent affairs in which the Phoenician women would ceaselessly repeat the word *adoni*. When the Greek writer Lucian visited Byblos in the second century AD he recorded the

ADONIS was killed and consigned to the underworld, but Aphrodite secured his release for half of each year, symbolizing the renewal of vegetation. (VENUS AND ADONIS BY ANTONIO CANOVA, MARBLE 1794.)

local belief that Adonis had been killed in a gorge. He also wrote that at the time of the god's return to the land of the living, pots of plants outside each house were tended to quickly blossom and wither, symbolizing Adonis's life and death. (See also *DYING AND RISING GODS*)

AGDISTIS was a hermaphrodite monster of Phrygian mythology. According to one tradition, he was born when some semen dropped from the great god Zeus on to Mount Ida, next to where the Great Mother *CYBELE* lay asleep.

The gods made Agdistis drunk by adding wine to the pool in which he bathed. The monster fell asleep, whereupon the gods tied his genitals to a tree. When he awoke and moved, he castrated himself and an almond or pomegranate tree grew from his sexual organs. One day Nana, the daughter of the river god gathered the fruit into her lap. One of the pieces of fruit disappeared, and the young woman discovered that she was pregnant. In due course, the nymph gave birth to *ATTIS*.

In one story, the adult Attis fell in love with a beautiful maiden. On the day of their wedding, Agdistis appeared at the feast in the form of the goddess Cybele. The maiden was furious to see Attis professing love to another woman and caused havoc. As a result, the bride died of self-inflicted wounds and Attis, mad with grief, castrated himself beneath a pine tree.

AGLIBOL was a moon god from Palmyra in northern Arabia. He was depicted with a sickle moon either on his forehead or on his shoulders. His name is sometimes said to mean "Bull of Bol", suggesting that the sickle was originally intended to represent bull's horns.

AHAT, or Aqhat, according to Phoenician mythology, was the son of a local ruler, Daniel. Daniel had no children, but, prompted by the rain and fertility god *BAAL*, the supreme god *EL* gave him a son. When Ahat grew up, the divine craftsman *KOTHAR* gave him a splendid bow made from twisted horns. The goddess *ANAT* longed to possess the weapon and tried to persuade Ahat to give it to her. When Ahat refused, the goddess promised him immortality but Ahat replied that humankind's destiny was to die. Anat then sent Yatpan, her attendant, to kill Ahat. Though Yatpan killed the hero, the bow was lost in the struggle. In punishment, Baal stopped the rains falling, and so the crops failed.

Daniel mourned his son's death for seven years. Although the end of the myth is lost, it is believed that Ahat was resurrected and fertility was restored to the land. Ahat thus probably came to be regarded as a dying and rising god.

AHRIMAN see *ANGRA MAINYU*.

AHURA MAZDA, or Ohrmazd, was the supreme god and "Wise Lord" of ancient Iran. He was regarded as the all-encompassing sky. Until the time of the great religious reformer *ZOROASTER*, who lived around 1200 BC, the Iranians worshipped numerous gods. Zoroaster denounced the old gods and Ahura Mazda came to be regarded as the one true creator god who was constantly beleaguered by *ANGRA MAINYU*, or Ahriman, the principle of darkness.

After creating the *AMESA SPENTAS* and *YAZATAS*, Ahura Mazda made people, cattle, fire, earth, sky, water and plants. Zoroaster taught that Ahura Mazda made light visible, so the god was often depicted as the sun.

Sometimes, however, the sun and moon are described as Ahura Mazda's eyes. Using the purifying quality of fire, Ahura Mazda was able to distinguish good from evil, and he bestowed fire, the symbol of truth, on his followers.

Under the Achaemenians, who ruled from 558 to 330 BC, Ahura Mazda was adopted as the patron of the royal house and was represented as a pair of vast wings. In the centuries following Zoroaster, a movement known as Zurvanism developed. Both Ahura Mazda and Angra Mainyu came to be regarded as descendants of *ZURVAN AKARANA*, or "Infinite Time". This helped to circumvent the problem of Ahura Mazda having created evil or, at least, having allowed it to exist. At the end of time, it was said that, "Ohrmazd will reign and will do everything according to his pleasure." (See also *ANGELS AND DJINN*)

AL-LAT, or Allat, was a pre-Islamic goddess of central and northern Arabia. Her following was

particularly pronounced at Ta'if near Mecca, where she was worshipped in the form of a block of white granite. Women in particular would circle the stone in Al-Lat's honour, perhaps because she was regarded as a type of mother goddess. Al-Lat represented the earth and was said to be one of the three daughters of *ALLAH*, the supreme god. She is also believed to have been associated with the sun, moon or the planet Venus.

AL-UZZA, or El-'Ozza, was an Arabian goddess of pre-Islamic times who was regarded by the Bedouin tribes of central Arabia as the youngest daughter of *ALLAH*, the supreme deity. She was worshipped in the form of a black stone, on the surface of which lay a mark or indentation called the "Impression of Aphrodite". Al-Uzza was said to live in a tree and was identified with the morning star. She formed the centre of a sacrificial cult, and archaeologists have discovered recent evidence that human sacrifice was offered to her.

The tribe to which the prophet Muhammad belonged showed particular reverence for the goddess. The prophet himself was said to have taken the sacred Black Stone of Islam and placed it in the *KA'ABA*, the shrine in Mecca, Islam's holiest city. The cult of Al-Uzza was served by priestesses and, even after the arrival of Islam, the Ka'aba's guardians still continued to be called "Sons of the Old Woman".

According to the Qur'an, the sacred book of Islam, Al-Uzza, together with Arabia's other principal goddesses, *AL-LAT* and *MANAT*, "are not names which ye have named, ye and your fathers, for which Allah hath revealed no warrant. They follow but a guess and that which they themselves desire." In northern Arabia, Al-Uzza was known as Han-Uzzai.

ALALU, according to the Hittites, was the first king of heaven who came from south of the Black Sea. One myth tells how Alalu sat upon his throne and "the mighty *ANU*, the first among the gods, stood before him, bowed down at his feet and handed him the cup to drink". After nine years, Alalu was deposed by Anu and fled to the earth – possibly the underworld. Anu was in turn dethroned by *KUMARBI*, who was overthrown by his son *TESHUB*, the weather god.

ALLAH was the supreme, though not sole, deity in Arabia before the arrival of Islam. He lived, together with other deities, in the heavens and was said to have created the earth and bestowed water on it. In pre-Islamic times, animism was prevalent throughout Arabia: trees and springs were worshipped and certain stones were believed to contain sacred power. However, the prophet Muhammad (c. AD 570–632) adopted Allah as the one true god, to whom total submission was due, and proclaimed it blasphemous to worship any other deity. According to the Qur'an, polytheism is the greatest sin.

Allah is said to be supreme and transcendent; he is regarded as the creator of all life, the controller of all nature, the bestower of bounty and the judge of humankind in the last days. Although Allah can be terrifying, he is none the less righteous, just and merciful.

Because Allah is believed to be completely different from everything he has created, it is forbidden for anyone to attempt to portray him. In the Qur'an, he is given 99 names. The hundredth and greatest name is known to no mortal.

ALLAT see *AL-LAT*.

THE AMESA SPENTAS, or the Amesha Spentas, are the holy immortals of Zoroastrianism. They probably belonged to the pantheon of ancient Iranian gods which

existed before *ZOROASTER*'s time. It is possible that, although the religious reformer denounced the old gods, he assimilated the Amesa Spentas into his teachings as aspects of *AHURA MAZDA*, the one and only true spirit set in opposition to *ANGRA MAINYU*, the spirit of evil.

The Amesa Spentas were said to serve Ahura Mazda, the "Supreme Lord". Otherwise known as Amshaspends or Ameshas Spenta, each of them ruled over a particular aspect of reality, such as a category of beings or a part of the year. *VOHU MANO* reigned over useful animals, including cattle. Asha-Vahishta looked after fire; Khshathra-Vairya moved the sun and heavens and ruled over metals; *SPENTA ARMAITI* ruled over the earth; Haurvatat governed the waters; and Ameretat governed plant life. Spenta Mainyu, who ruled over humanity, is either numbered among the Amesa Spentas or identified as Ahura Mazda himself.

AMON, wearing his plumed headdress, protects the young pharaoh, Tutankhamun, who reinstated him at the head of the Egyptian pantheon. (1350 BC.)

AMESHA SPENTAS see *AMESA SPENTAS*.

AMON, the Egyptian "King of the Gods", first came to prominence as the god of Thebes in Upper Egypt, where he was worshipped as a fertility deity. He grew in importance to become the god who looked after the most splendid of the *PHAROAHS*. Amon was often depicted wearing a headdress surmounted by two plumes, or sometimes with the head of a ram.

By the 18th dynasty, in the second millennium BC, Amon had become the supreme god of the whole of Egypt and was identified with the sun god as Amon-Ra, although *RA* continued to have his own separate following. The pharaohs Thuthmosis III and Amenhotep III described themselves as "Sons of Amon" and claimed that the god brought them victory over their enemies.

During the reign of Amenhotep's son, Akhenaten, worship of Amon was forbidden while *ATEN* was declared the true god. However, in 1361 BC, the succeeding pharaoh reinstated Amon and called himself Tutankhamun or "Living Image of

Amon". Worship of Amon eventually spread beyond Egypt into Ethiopia and Libya. Amon's wife was Mut, whose son was called Khons.

AN see *ANU*.

ANAHITA, the Iranian goddess of water and fertility, was widely worshipped in Achaemenian times (558–330 BC) and was often associated with the great god *MITHRA*. In the fourth century BC, the ruler Artaxerxes II ordered that images of Anahita should be erected in all the principal cities of the empire. Her following later spread throughout Asia Minor and the West.

Anahita assisted *SPENTA ARMAITI* and was associated with *HAOMA*, the god who conferred immortality. Occasionally identified with the planet Venus, she is said to have originated from *ISHTAR*, the Babylonian fertility deity who is associated with the same planet. Her name means "Immaculate".

Anahita was often represented dressed in gleaming gold with a crown and jewels. The dove and peacock were her sacred creatures, and sacred prostitution formed part of her cult.

ANAHITA, the Iranian patroness of women and fertility, and an aspect of the "Great Goddess", crowns the ruler Narses. (BAS-RELIEF, LATE 3RD CENTURY BC.)

ANGRA MAINYU was the Zoroastrian principle of darkness, the antagonist of Ahura Mazda. He tried to thwart Ahura Mazda's plans to create an earthly paradise by sowing doubt and discord in the world, and even sought to destroy humanity. (GOLD MEDALLION FROM THE OXUS TREASURE, C. 5TH CENTURY BC.)

ANAT, or Anath, was a goddess of the Canaanites and Phoenicians, and was the sister, and sometimes the consort, of *BAAL*. Her name is usually translated as "Providence" or "Precaution".

The goddess had a reputation for violence. According to one myth, she slaughtered Baal's worshippers and only ceased her attack when Baal promised to reveal the secret of lightning to her. Anat later asked the supreme god, *EL,* to give Baal a house, but it was the great mother goddess *ASTARTE* who eventually persuaded him to do so. After moving into the splendid palace, Baal boasted that he was now omnipotent and challenged *MOT*, the god of death, to a contest. However, it was Anat who eventually destroyed Mot, by killing, thrashing and burning him.

Anat was later assimilated into the Egyptian pantheon, where she was regarded as a goddess of war and a daughter of the sun god *RA*.

The Egyptians usually depicted her carrying a spear, axe and shield, and wearing a tall crown surmounted by two ostrich feathers.

ANATH see *ANAT.*

ANBAY was a pre-Islamic god of southern Arabia who was known as the "Lord of Justice". Famed for his oracle, he spoke on behalf of the moon god, Amm, who ranked above him in the pantheon.

ANGRA MAINYU, or Ahriman, was the principle of darkness in ancient Iranian mythology. He was set in opposition to *AHURA MAZDA*, the principle of goodness and truth. Ahura Mazda planned to make Iran into an earthly paradise, but Angra Mainyu interfered, creating harsh weather conditions, smoke, darkness, sickness, disease and all manner of other evils. His was a world of death in which summer lasted for only two months whereas winter lasted for ten. Where people had faith, Angra Mainyu sowed the seeds of doubt,

ANAT, the sister and sometimes the consort of Baal, was a Phoenician goddess with a reputation for violence. She later became a part of the Egyptian pantheon as a goddess of war. (ASSYRIAN SEAL.)

and where there were riches, he created laziness and poverty. Such was the extent of his evil-doing that he was sometimes accused of having killed *GEUSH URVAN*, the primeval bull. Angra Mainyu's symbol was the snake.

In later times, during the reign of the Sassanian kings (AD 226–652), the idea of *ZURVAN AKARANA,* or "Infinite Time" was developed. Both Angra Mainyu and Ahura Mazda were regarded as the offspring of Zurvan Akarana, who was said to have promised authority to the firstborn. As a result, Angra Mainyu tore his way out of the womb before his brother and held the reins of power for several thousand years. However, Zoroastrians believe that there will come a day when Ahura Mazda will succeed to power and Angra Mainyu will be destroyed, sinking into eternal darkness.

ANSHAR was the male principle in Babylonian mythology. In the Babylonian epic *Enuma Elish* ("When on High"), he and Kishar, the female principle, are described as the second pair of deities, following Lahmu and Lahamu, the first divine couple. Both these couples originated when *APSU*, the primeval sweet water, mingled with *TIAMAT*, the primeval salt water. It is generally believed that the name Anshar means "Horizon of Heaven" and that the god represented the celestial world; Kishar, on the other hand, is thought to have been a terrestrial deity whose name means "Horizon of Earth".

Anshar and Kishar begat *ANU*, the sky god, and *EA*, the god of fresh water and wisdom. They also

ANSHAR was a primordial deity of Babylonian mythology who represented the male principle. He was eventually equated with Ashur, a warrior god who ensured the victories of the Assyrians.

begat the Igigi, the deities who inhabited the sky, and the Anunnake, the gods who lived on earth and in the underworld. From the ninth century BC onwards, Assur or Ashur, the national god of Assyria, was equated with Anshar.

ANU was the son of *ANSHAR* and Kishar, the male and female principles of Babylonian mythology. He formed one of a triad of creator gods which also included *EA*, the god of sweet and fertilizing waters, and *ENLIL* or Bel, lord of the wind.

The god of the sky, Anu was the supreme deity who reigned over the heavens. He was known as the father of the gods and had the power to judge those who committed misdeeds after summoning them before his throne, in front of which were placed the sceptre, the diadem, the crown and the staff of command. The stars were Anu's soldiers, whom he had created in order to destroy the wicked. He never descended to earth and had little to do with human beings. Rather, he stayed in the heavens and busied himself with the fate of the universe. In Sumerian mythology, Anu was known as An. He was sometimes represented by a crown on a throne.

Anu was introduced into the Hittite pantheon from Mesopotamia by way of the Hurrians. In the story of the divine kingship, *ALALU*, the king of heaven, was served by Anu, the first among the gods. Alalu reigned for nine years until Anu deposed him. After another nine years, Anu's minister *KUMARBI* seized the throne. Anu immediately flew up into the sky, but Kumarbi seized him by the foot and bit off his penis. However, Anu's semen impregnated Kumarbi and gave rise to three mighty gods, who are believed to be different aspects of the weather god, *TESHUB*.

ANUBIS was originally said to be the fourth son of the Egyptian sun god, *RA*. However, in later times, he came to be regarded as the child of the vegetation god, *OSIRIS,* and *NEPHTHYS,* the sister of *ISIS.* When Anubis was born, Nephthys hid the child in the marshes of the Nile delta in order to protect him from her consort *SETH.* The infant god was discovered there by Isis, the mother goddess, who subsequently brought him up.

When Osiris left Egypt in order to spread his teachings throughout the world, Anubis accompanied him on his travels. Later, when Osiris was killed by Seth, Anubis organized his burial, binding him with cloth and thereby creating the first mummy. As a result, Anubis came to be regarded as the inventor of funeral rites and was referred to as "Lord of the Mummy Wrappings". The god also assisted in the judgment of the dead and guided the honest dead towards the throne of Osiris. Anubis was depicted either as a jackal or as a man with the head of a jackal. (See also *GATEWAYS TO THE GODS; UNDERWORLDS*)

APEP was the eternal enemy of *RA*, the supreme god of the Egyptian pantheon. A terrifying serpent, Apep symbolized chaos and destruction. Each day, as the sun god, Ra, crossed the sky in his boat, Apep would viciously attack the vessel and occasionally, during a total eclipse, he was believed to have swallowed it whole.

Despite his ferocity, Apep never gained total victory over his enemy. However, at the same time, he himself was never believed to have been finally and completely conquered. However, the reddening of the sky at dusk was said to demonstrate that the serpent had been overcome by the sun's strength. According to one story, Apep was

ANU, Babylonian god of the sky, and Enlil, god of the earth, are symbolized by horned crowns on stylized thrones. (DETAIL OF BABYLONIAN BOUNDARY STONE, C. 1120 BC.)

created when *NEITH*, the "Great Mother" associated with war and hunting, spat into *NUN*, the primal watery chaos. In later times, Apep came to be identified with *SETH*. He is often known by the Greek name of Apophis. (See also *SERPENTS AND DRAGONS*)

APEP was the Egyptian symbol of chaos, a giant snake who occupied the Duat or underworld. The sun god, Ra, represented here as a falcon, battled daily with the snake. (SMALL LIMESTONE PYRAMID, 19TH DYNASTY.)

SACRED ANIMALS

SURROUNDED BY A HOSTILE, DESERT landscape, people and animals alike depended on the great rivers that provided water and fertile soil. The ancient Egyptians were forcefully reminded of their close kinship with the animal world, as they had to share the fertile flood plain of the Nile with dangerous, powerful creatures such as lions, crocodiles, hippopotamuses and snakes. The association of these animals with the life-giving force of the river, and the fear and respect they commanded, gave rise to animal cults, which reached their peak during the Late and Ptolemaic Periods from 664–30 BC. Devotees did not worship the animals themselves but associated their qualities with a particular deity, who was portrayed in animal form. At shrines, offerings consisted of small animal figurines or mummified creatures. The temple officials turned this into a profitable business, breeding huge numbers of animals for mummification and sale to worshippers. The catacombs at North Saqqara, for instance, are thought to hold approximately four million mummified ibis (wading birds), dedicated to the god Thoth.

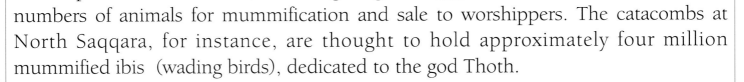

THE COBRA (left), or uraeus, rearing defensively, was a symbol that was both protective and potentially dangerous. The snake accompanied the deceased on his or her journey to the underworld in the sacred boat, and similar images were also placed protectively around shrines. A rearing female cobra formed part of the pharaoh's regalia, worn on the forehead, where it symbolically guarded both the pharaoh and the country. The Eye of Horus, a god often depicted with the head of a falcon, was another guarantee of protection in the afterlife. (DETAIL FROM A BOOK OF THE DEAD, 21ST DYNASTY, HERUBEN PAPYRUS, C. 1000 BC.)

BASTET (above) was the daughter (or sometimes sister and consort) of the Egyptian sun god, Ra. She was originally a fierce and vengeful goddess, portrayed as a lioness, but from around 1000 BC she became more peaceable and took on the shape of a cat. She was a goddess of fertility and love, and protected her devotees against disease and evil spirits. Her principal place of worship was at Bubastis, where thousands of mummified cats were dedicated to her. In the name of the goddess, cats were loved and respected by the Egyptians, to the extent that the killing of a cat was an offence punishable by death. (EGYPTIAN BRONZE, 6TH CENTURY BC.)

RA-HERARHTY (below), god of the rising sun, symbolized by his falcon wings and sun-disc headdress, is carved on the polished granite capstone of the pyramid of Amenemhet III. Coiled around the sun disc is the symbol of the cobra goddess Wadjet, representing the pharaoh's royal authority and power over the life and death of his people. The carvings below include a bee and an ibis, representing Thoth, the wise counsellor of the gods and the judge of the dead. (PYRAMIDION, C. 1818–1772 BC.)

APIS (above), the sacred bull, was worshipped as a living animal believed to be the reincarnation of the god Ptah at his temple at Memphis. Mythical bulls, symbols of strength and potency, occurred in many belief systems from the earliest times. Hathor, the Egyptian goddess of maternal and sexual love, took the form of a cow (above right) who nourished humankind with her milk. She was the protector of women, helping them to conceive and give birth, and was regarded as the mother of the pharaohs. (EGYPTIAN BRONZE, 7TH–6TH CENTURY BC.)

DRAGONS (right) symbolized Marduk, the tutelary god of the fabled city of Babylon. These composite creatures had the head and tail of a serpent, the body and forelegs of a lion and the hind legs of a falcon, and were emblazoned on the monumental Ishtar Gate at the climax of the ceremonial route through the city. The processional way was lined with rows of lions sacred to Ishtar, the goddess of love and fertility. (GLAZED BRICK RELIEF, 6TH CENTURY BC.)

KHNUM (above), the ram-headed god, took mud from the life-giving Nile and used it to create humanity on his potter's wheel. He was also responsible for supervising the annual flooding of the river. At his sanctuary near its mythical source, offerings of mummified rams decorated with gold leaf were buried in stone tombs. His consort was Satis, who was depicted pouring water on to the dry earth.

SEBEK (left), the crocodile god, represented the skill and strength of the pharaoh in battle. The qualities he needed to display could be seen in the crocodiles of the Nile, which inspired awe with their speed and agility in catching their prey and the fearsome strength of their jaws. The mortuary goddess Serket took the form of a scorpion, though she was sometimes depicted in human form with a scorpion headdress. Her role was to guard the canopic jars containing the vital organs of the dead, and to protect the throne of the pharaoh. (EGYPTIAN BRONZES, 6TH CENTURY BC.)

APIS, or Hapi, was the most renowned of Egypt's sacred animals. He was worshipped at Memphis, where his temple lay opposite that of the great creator god *PTAH*. Apis, in the form of a real black bull, was believed to be the reincarnation or "glorious soul" of Ptah, who was said to have inseminated a virgin cow in the form of fire, and to have been born again as a black bull.

Each day, Apis was let loose in the courtyard attached to his temple, and the priests would use his movements as a means for divining the future. Usually, the Apis bull was allowed to die of old age, but he was drowned in a fountain if he reached the age of 25. The bull was twice assassinated by the Persians.

Ptah's priests were said to be able to recognize the next holy bull by discovering certain markings on the creature's body, including a white triangle on his forehead and a crescent moon on his right side. The extent of the reverence with which the sacred bulls were regarded can be gauged by the fact that their mummified bodies were buried with great ceremony in huge underground burial chambers. (See also *SACRED ANIMALS*)

APSU, in Mesopotamian mythology, was the watery abyss or primordial, fresh-water ocean, which existed at the beginning of time and which circled and supported the earth. Apsu spread happiness and abundance over the earth and was the source of knowledge and wisdom. Eventually, the waters of Apsu merged with those of *TIAMAT*, the primordial, salt-water ocean, and gave rise to Mummu, the waves, and the primal couple, Lahmu and Lahamu. *ANSHAR* and Kishar, the next divine couple to arise from the waves, were the male and female principles who bore the great gods *ANU* and *EA* as well as the other divinities who peopled the sky, the earth and the underworld.

In time, Apsu became troubled by the gods and plotted with Tiamat to destroy them. Tiamat was at first unwilling to take part in the battle, but, when Apsu was slain by the god Ea, she was prompted to seek revenge. Ea's son, the great god *MARDUK*, who had been born in the waters of Apsu, was chosen to challenge Tiamat. The bloody battle that ensued gave rise to the creation of the world and the sky. According to one tradition in Sumerian mythology, the goddess Nammu formed the first men from clay dug out of the waters of Apsu. In the epic of *GILGAMESH*, the hero descended into the waters of Apsu to find the plant of eternal life.

AQHAT see *AHAT*.

ARINNA was the name of a Hittite town. Its chief goddess was known as the "Sun of Arinna", or Ariniddu. The "Queen of Heaven and Earth", the goddess Arinna became the supreme patroness of the Hittite kingdom, protecting it from enemies and helping out in time of war. Her symbol was the sun disc. Arinna was identified with the Hurrian goddess *HEPAT*; both deities were said to be married to the weather god *TESHUB*.

The sun goddess Arinna was sometimes addressed as a masculine deity, the "Inspired Lord of Justice". The sun god was also an important figure in Hittite mythology, although his actual name has been lost. He was regarded as the king of the gods and a dispenser of truth and justice. In one prayer he was addressed as "Sun god of heaven, my lord, shepherd of mankind! Thou risest, O sun-god of heaven, from the sea and goest up to heaven. O sun-god of heaven, my lord, daily thou sittest in judgment upon man, dog, pig, and the wild beasts of the field." There was also a sun god of the water and a sun god of the underworld, through which the sun was believed to travel during the night.

ARSU see *RUDA*.

ASHERAT; ASHTORETH see *ASTARTE*

ASHUR see *ANSHAR*.

ASTARTE was the principal goddess of the Phoenicians and Canaanites. She was incorporated into Egyptian mythology as a daughter either of the sun god *RA,* or of *PTAH,* and she was often depicted naked, bearing weapons and riding a horse.

According to one story from Egyptian mythology, Ptah and the other great gods were forced to pay tributes to the sea. Gifts of silver, gold and precious stones were brought to the seashore, but the sea wanted more. The gods then

ASTARTE was the principal goddess of the Phoenicians and the Canaanites. This figurine shows her, perhaps, as a fertility deity. She was associated with love and procreation. (CERAMIC FIGURINE, GATH, 8TH–7TH CENTURIES BC.)

told Astarte to take more offerings to the sea. When she arrived at the shore, Astarte mocked the sea, who responded by insisting that he have Astarte herself as a gift. The great gods covered Astarte with jewels and sent her back to the shore, but this time *SETH* accompanied her in order to fight the sea. Although the end of the story is missing, it is usually presumed that Seth fought the sea, and saved Astarte.

The name Astarte is sometimes translated as "Womb", or "That Which Issues from the Womb",

ATEN, the sun god, is symbolized by a sun disc whose rays fall on the pharaoh Akhenaten and queen Nefertiti as they perform a sacrifice to him. (FLAT RELIEF, AMARNA, C. 1350 BC.)

and Astarte the light, heavenly aspect. In one text, they are both described as the daughters of *NEITH*, an Egyptian mother goddess. Moreover, they were both known as "Lady of Heaven". Aphrodite is widely believed to have developed from Astarte.

ATAR, or "Fire", was said to be the son of the Iranian deity *AHURA MAZDA*, although fire worship probably existed long before the naming of the supreme being. According to the teachings of Zoroastrianism, fire was one of Ahura Mazda's seven creations. Atar was said to bring men comfort and wisdom, and to defend the world from evil. It represented the light of truth and the divine spark in humankind, which signified the presence of the supreme god.

The monstrous dragon *AZHI DAHAKA* sought to extinguish the divine fire in a bloody battle, which took place across land, sea and air. Eventually, Atar caught the dragon and chained it to a mountain.

ATEN was a sun god who came to pre-eminence in the 14th century BC under Amenhotep IV, a *PHARAOH* of the 18th dynasty. He was regarded as none other than the sun god *RA* himself.

Amenhotep IV built temples to Aten close to those of the supreme god *AMON* and, to the disgust of Amon's priests, piled Aten's temples high with gifts. Four years into his reign, the pharaoh pronounced that the religion of Aten was the only official faith and that the god was to be worshipped as the exclusive creator of humankind. Worship of all other gods – especially Amon – was forbidden.

In an attempt to spread the religion of Aten throughout the empire, Amon's temples were closed and his images defaced. The pharaoh changed his name from Amenhotep, meaning "Amon is Satisfied", to Akhenaten, "Glory of Aten" or "He Who is Devoted to Aten", and relocated his capital from Thebes to a city known today as el-Armana, which he had built specifically to glorify Aten.

Aten is always depicted as an enormous red disc, from which rays of light emanate. The rays, ending in hands, were believed to extend the beauty of Aten to the ruler. When Akhenaten died, Amon and the other gods were reinstated, and Aten's rays were sliced through to prevent his beauty reaching Akhenaten.

ATEN, the sun-disc, was worshipped by the pharoah Akhenaten as the embodiment of the supreme force of light, and, during his reign, worship of all the other deities of the Egyptian pantheon was forbidden. His successor, Tutankhamun (below) restored the old gods. (CARVED WOOD, 14TH CENTURY BC.)

suggesting that the goddess was primarily a fertility deity. Astarte was also associated with love and procreation, and her cult included the practice of temple prostitution among her devotees.

In the Old Testament of the Bible, she appears as Ashtoreth, and *SOLOMON* had a temple built in her honour near Jerusalem. Indeed, the Israelites sometimes revered the goddess as the queen of heaven and wife of *YAHWEH*.

The goddess Asherat, or Ashera-of-the-Sea, tends to be viewed as identical with Astarte. She was called "Mother of the Gods" and was said to have had 70 children. According to texts dating from the 14th century BC, the supreme god *EL* took two women, generally believed to be Asherat and *ANAT*, as

his consorts, and by them fathered *SHACHAR* and Shalim, "Dawn" and "Dusk", and many other deities.

It is still not certain whether Anat and Astarte were two separate goddesses or different aspects of the same goddess. Anat may have been the dark aspect of the goddess

21

ATTAR was worshipped in southern Arabia in pre-Islamic times. A god of war, he was often referred to as "He who is Bold in Battle". One of his symbols was the spear-point, and the antelope was his sacred animal. He had power over Venus, the morning star, and was believed to provide humankind with water.

ATTIS was the consort of *CYBELE*, the great mother goddess of Phrygia in Asia Minor. A vegetation god, he was sometimes known as Papas, or "Father". One of the oldest stories concerning the birth of Attis tells how the hermaphrodite *AGDISTIS* fell asleep, whereupon the gods tied its genitals to a tree. Agdistis awoke with a start, and the severed genitals fell to the ground. An almond tree grew up on the spot, and in due course Nana, the daughter of the river god, became pregnant by one of its fruits. The girl eventually gave birth to Attis. Other legends say that the god was a foundling or the son of a king.

The best-known story of Attis is that in which his desperate love for Cybele drove him insane, leading him to castrate himself under a pine tree. Flowers and trees grew up from his blood. Although he died, the god was reborn and united with Cybele.

The cult of Cybele spread to Greece and Rome, and with it, that of Attis. Cybele was said to have fallen in love with Attis, who was regarded as a handsome young shepherd. She chose him as her priest and imposed a vow of chastity upon him. However, Attis fell in love with a river nymph, so Cybele caused him to suffer a fit of madness, during which he mutilated himself. When the god recovered, he was about to kill himself when Cybele changed him into a fir tree. In another version of the story, Attis was gored to death by a boar sent by Zeus.

Each spring, at the end of March, a five-day festival was held in honour of Attis. The first day was

ATTIS was a vegetation god in Phrygia in Asia Minor. His death and rebirth symbolized the natural cycle. In a Roman legend, Attis was gored to death by a boar sent by Zeus. (MARBLE BUST, IMPERIAL ROME.)

one of mourning. The god, represented by a sacred fir tree taken from the grove near Cybele's temple, was bound with bandages, decorated with ribbons and flowers, and carried through the streets. On the second day, Cybele's priests performed frenzied dances, and on the third day they castrated themselves, sprinkling the altar and effigy of Attis with their blood. The fourth day was that on which the resurrection of Attis was celebrated. The fifth day was one of rest. A ritual marriage between Cybele and Attis formed part of the ceremony, with Cybele's high priest taking the role of the god.

The Romans generally represented Attis as a shepherd, usually holding a shepherd's crook and sometimes carrying a sheep on his shoulders. He plays a pipe and wears a pointed cap on his head. The rays of the sun, or ears of corn, protrude from the cap, symbolizing his function as a god of regeneration and rebirth. (See also *DYING AND RISING GODS*)

AZHI DAHAKA, the monstrous dragon of ancient Iranian mythology, was said to have had three heads, six eyes and three pairs of fangs. He was sometimes regarded as a mythical king of Babylon,

B

Iran's enemy, or as the enemy of *YIMA*, the great king. Originally, Azhi Dahaka was believed to kill cattle and men. One story tells how the hero *FERIDUN* cut the creature open with his sword and was horrified to find lizards and toads pouring out of its insides.

In time, Azhi Dahaka came to be seen as the embodiment of falsehood and the servant of *ANGRA MAINYU*, the principle of darkness. *ATAR*, the fire god, went into battle against the monster and harried him through land, sea and air before finally catching him and chaining him to a mountain.

It was believed that at the end of time Azhi Dahaka would succeed in breaking free from his chains and ravage the earth again. Eventually, the hero *KERESASPA* would kill the monster. (See also *SERPENTS AND DRAGONS*)

THE BA AND KA were believed by the ancient Egyptians to be the soul and spirit, or vital essence, of a dead person. The Ba hovered over the deceased and was usually depicted as a bird with a human head. The Ka was said to appear to the deceased in the form of a blue phoenix and was believed to return to the tomb, where it ate food left by relatives and priests. So deeply entrenched was this belief that menus were sometimes inscribed on the walls of tombs.

BAAL was the name given by many Canaanite tribes to their chief gods. In the Bible his name is used as a synonym for "false god, and sacrifice to him is there condemned". (ILLUSTRATION FROM MYTHS OF BABYLONIA AND ASSYRIA BY LEWIS SPENCE.)

BAAL, meaning "Lord" or "Owner", was the name given by many Canaanite tribes to their chief god. When the Israelites entered the land of Canaan, they took up the word and used it to describe any alien god – it is as a general term for a "false god" that the name Baal is used in the Bible. The most renowned Baal of Canaanite mythology was the rain and fertility god associated with the storm god, Hadad. He lived on a mountain in the north of the region and was sometimes referred to as "Lord of the North".

One story tells how this Baal defeated *YAM*, the sea deity. Yam asked the supreme god *EL* to crown him king. El agreed but warned him that first of all he would have to defeat Baal. Learning of the forthcoming battle, Baal equipped himself with magic weapons made by the gods, and as a result, he succeeded in killing Yam and scattering his remains. Baal then proclaimed himself king, built a sumptuous dwelling place on Mount Saphon and took control of several cities.

After this victory, Baal became so proud that he decided to challenge *MOT*, the god of death. He forced Mot to live in the barren wastelands and barred him from all fertile regions. In response, Mot challenged Baal to come to his underground dwelling and eat mud, the food of the dead. Baal took up the challenge and died.

BAAL was said to have a voice like thunder, and that he watered the earth through a hole in the floor of his palace. In the Greco-Roman period, Baal became assimilated in the Palestine region with Zeus and Jupiter. (GILDED BRONZE, SYRIA, C. 14-15TH CENTURY)

All the gods mourned Baal's death. His wife, the ferocious *ANAT*, descended to the underworld to retrieve his corpse. However, she was unable to revive Baal and so appealed to Mot for help. When Mot refused to come to her aid, Anat burst into a frenzy and slaughtered him, whereupon Baal returned to life. Baal is thus seen as a dying and rising god. He is often depicted wielding a thunderbolt, or a flash of lightning. (See also *DYING AND RISING GODS*)

C

BASAMUM was worshipped in southern Arabia in pre-Islamic times. His name may come from the Arabic word for a balsam bush, suggesting that he was a god of healing. One ancient text tells how the god cured two wild goats.

BASTET was the local goddess of Bubastis, or "House of Bastet", the capital of a province of Lower Egypt. She was usually regarded as the daughter of the sun god *RA*, although she was sometimes said to be his sister and consort. Later, she became the wife of the creator god *PTAH*. According to some accounts, it was Bastet, rather

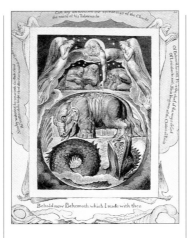

Cut ony tenderness the spreading of thy Clouds the name of his Tabernacle

Behold now Behemoth which I made with thee

than *NEPHTHYS*, who was the mother of the jackal-headed god *ANUBIS*.

Originally a lioness goddess symbolizing both the warmth of the sun and the rage of the sun god's eye, from about 1000 BC Bastet came to be represented as a cat, or a cat-headed woman. However, in some stories she continued to possess the qualities of Sekhmet (see *HATHOR)*, the lion-headed goddess. Usually a benevolent goddess, Bastet protected humanity from diseases and evil spirits. Most importantly, she was a goddess of fertility, sex and love, and enjoyed music and dancing. In the fourth century BC fertility festivals were held in her honour at her temple at Bubastis. Cats were venerated as Bastet's sacred animals, and their mummified bodies were buried at her sanctuaries. (See also *SACRED ANIMALS*)

BEHEMOTH was a terrifying monster of Hebrew mythology, the dry-land equivalent of the monstrous sea serpent *LEVIATHAN*. According to the Old Testament

BASTET (left) was usually portrayed as either a cat or a cat-headed woman. Originally a local goddess of Bubastis, her cult reached its height in the Late and Ptolemaic periods (c 660–30 BC) when animal cults became a major feature of popular religion. Bronze figurines and mummified cats were given as offerings. (BRONZE, C. 5TH CENTURY BC.)

BEHEMOTH (left) and the sea monster Leviathan were used in the Book of Job as examples of the largest and strongest animals imaginable. (HAND-TINTED ENGRAVING BY WILLIAM BLAKE, C. 1793.)

Book of Job, Behemoth was associated with the hippopotamus. The monster is sometimes said to have developed from *TIAMAT*, the fearsome Babylonian goddess.

BEL see *ENLIL*.

BELILI see *TAMMUZ*.

BORAK (below) with a human head, the body of a winged horse and a peacock's tail, carries the prophet Muhammad to heaven, surrounded by winged peris. (QAJAR LACQUERWORK, C. 1870.)

BORAK was a fabulous beast of Islamic mythology. Part human, part animal, the prophet Muhammad was said to have ridden on its back on the night of his ascension to heaven. The creature's name means "Lightning".

CORYBANTES see *KORYBANTES*.

CYBELE was the great mother and fertility goddess of Phrygian mythology. She probably originated as a mountain goddess and was sometimes referred to as the "Lady of Ida", a mountain in western Anatolia. She inhabited the wild and dangerous regions of the earth and ruled over the fiercest of wild animals. Cybele's origins have

CYBELE (above) was the great mother of Phrygian mythology. She was associated with the earth and with a black stone – believed to be a meteorite – which was enshrined at Pergamum. (2ND CENTURY AD.)

CYBELE's (right) priests, the Galli, celebrated rites in her honour which included music, convulsive dances, sacrifices and voluntary self-mutilation. (ROMAN CARVING, 1ST–3RD CENTURY AD.)

sometimes been traced back as far as Çatal Höyük, a large Neolithic site in southern Anatolia. There, archaeologists unearthed a terracotta figure believed to be the mother goddess in the act of giving birth.

Cybele was primarily associated with the earth, and in particular with a black stone enshrined at Pergamum. Other cities where worship of the great mother was particularly fervent were Troy and Pessinus. In Phrygia, Cybele may originally have been known as KUBABA, or "Lady of the Cube". She is sometimes associated with an ancient goddess of that name who was worshipped at Carchemish in the Hittite empire. The shrines of both goddesses were situated in caves or near rocks.

The cult of Cybele eventually spread from Asia Minor to Greece. In the fifth century BC, a magnificent statue of the goddess flanked by lions was placed in her temple in Athens. In 204 BC, the black stone sacred to Cybele was brought from Phrygia to Rome. An oracle had foretold that if the "Phrygian Mother" were brought from Pergamum, she would aid the Romans in their war against the Carthaginians.

At Cybele's annual celebrations, held in spring, a chariot harnessed to lions would be drawn through the streets of Rome. According to the historian Lucretius (99–55 BC): "Borne from her sacred precinct in her car she drove a yoke of lions; her head they wreathed with a battlemented crown, because

embattled on glorious heights she sustains towns; and dowered with this emblem even now the image of the divine mother is carried in awesome state through great countries. On her the diverse nations in the ancient rite of worship call as the Mother of Ida, and they give her Phrygian bands to bear her company, because from those lands first they say corn began to be produced throughout the whole world."

The public rites of Cybele were orgiastic and ecstatic. Her priests, the Galli or Galloi, would beat and castrate themselves in mad frenzies of passion, using whips decorated with knuckle bones. The celebrations were accompanied by the sacrifice of a bull or ram, during which the initiate, or high priest or priestess of Cybele, stood beneath

a platform and was drenched in the blood of the sacrificed animal. Cybele's followers believed that her mysteries would lead them to be reborn after death in a new life.

Cybele's attributes are a mirror, a pomegranate and a key. The great myth attached to the goddess is that in which she takes vengeance on ATTIS for his infidelity and causes him to go mad, to castrate himself and to die. Eventually, however, she gives him back his life. According to another story, Cybele and Gordius, the king of Phrygia, had a son whom they called Midas. This was the Midas who, after wishing that everything he touched might turn to gold, found himself unable to eat or drink until the god Dionysus took pity on him.

D

THE DAEVAS were gods in the Indo-Aryan period of ancient Iran. The religious reformer ZOROASTER initially regarded them as unimportant, but he later came to view them as enemies of the true religion. Whereas the DRUJS were usually female, most daevas were male. ANGRA MAINYU or Ahriman, the principle of darkness, was said to rule over the demons. They specialized in trickery and deceit, and in putting obstacles in the way of all efforts to achieve good.

Many of the daevas stood in direct opposition to one of the AMESA SPENTAS, or "Holy Immortals". One demon would lie in wait on the Chinvat Bridge, which souls had to cross in order to reach AHURA MAZDA's paradise. If the creature caught them, he would throw them into the depths below. Another demon attempted to persuade rulers to be tyrannical, and a third promoted pride and rebellion. Some demons brought about old age and senility, and others caused rage and devastation.

The great hero RUSTEM constantly fought demons. In one story, a demon called Arzang attacked, captured and blinded the king. Rustem finally managed to release the ruler and to restore his eyesight using the heart of a demon as medicine.

In Armenian mythology, the daevas were known as devs. The daevas continued to be revered as good spirits in India.

DAGAN, the chief god of the Philistines, may have been a sea god and was represented with the tail of a fish.

DANIEL was preserved in the lions' den by an angel sent from Yahweh. (MOSAIC, HOSIOS LOUKAS, GREECE, 11TH CENTURY.)

DAGAN was a god of corn and fertility who was worshipped in both Canaan and Mesopotamia. The deity was often regarded as the father of BAAL, the god of rain and fertility. Several kings of Akkad and Babylonia declared themselves to be "Sons of Dagan", including King Hammurabi and Ashurnasirpal II.

In the Old Testament, a god called Dagon is described as the chief god of the Philistines. Samson destroyed Dagon's temple at Gaza by pulling down its two main pillars. This Dagon may have been a sea god, and he was represented with the tail of a fish. However, there continues to be some dispute as to whether Dagan and Dagon are one and the same deity.

DAGON see DAGAN.

DANIEL appears in the Old Testament as a prisoner in the sixth century BC of the Babylonian king Nebuchadnezzar. In 597 BC, the king seized Jerusalem. A decade later, the city was attacked, and the Hebrews were taken to Babylon where they were held in captivity until the city fell. Daniel was one of these Hebrew exiles. He gained a reputation for interpreting dreams and visions, earning the title "Master of Magicians", and was made a provincial ruler. However, Nebuchadnezzar commanded all his subjects to worship an image of gold. Shadrach, Meschach and Abednego, Daniel's friends, refused to do so, insisting on remaining true to YAHWEH. The king threw the men into a fiery furnace but astonishingly, they remained unharmed.

Nebuchadnezzar had many troubling dreams and called on Daniel to interpret them for him. According to Daniel, the dreams meant that Nebuchadnezzar would be banished from Babylon. The prophecy came true, and in the king's absence, his son Belshazzar ruled the kingdom. One evening, during a magnificent feast that Belshazzar was holding for a thousand of his lords, mysterious writing appeared on the palace wall: "In the same hour came forth fingers of a man's hand and wrote over against the candlestick upon the plaister of the wall of the king's palace." Daniel took the message to mean that Babylon would be conquered by the Medes and Persians. In due course, Darius the Median did indeed take the kingdom from Belshazzar.

Members of the new court became envious of Daniel's position and powers. They devised a plot whereby the king was forced to have Daniel thrown into a den of lions. Darius sealed the entrance of the den with a stone, but Yahweh sent an angel to Daniel's aid, forcing the lions to close their mouths: "So Daniel was taken up out of the den, and no manner of hurt was found upon him, because he believed in his God."

THE DEVIL see SATAN.

THE DJINN, according to Arabic and Islamic belief, are usually ugly and evil demons with supernatural powers. In pre-Islamic belief, the djinn were nature spirits who were said to be capable of driving people mad. They roamed the wild and lonely desert areas and, though usually invisible, they were able to take on any shape, whether animal or human.

In Islamic lore, the djinn were modified. They were an intermediate creation, coming between humankind and the angels. Those that refused to believe in Islam became demons, whereas others became beautiful and good spirits.

King *SOLOMON* was said to have tamed numerous djinn and to have become their ruler with the help of his magic ring. He allegedly carried them on his back when he travelled and ordered them to build the Temple at Jerusalem, as well as beautiful gardens and palaces.

There were several kinds of djinn, each with different degrees of power. The ghouls were female spirits who lived in the wilderness and manifested themselves as animals. *IBLIS*, or *SATAN*, is often regarded as the chief djinnee.

Djinn are born from smokeless fire. They are often said to live with other supernatural beings in the Kaf, a mythical range of mountains that encircles the earth. (See also *ANGELS AND DJINN*)

THE DRUJS, according to ancient Iranian mythology, were the enemies of the *asha*, the universal law. The monstrous, demonic beings, usually female, made every effort to further the course of evil. The horrific dragon or snake *AZHI DAHAKA* was one of their number, as was Nasu, who was said to settle on dead bodies in the form of a fly with the intention of hastening their decay. The druj Jahi was a symbol of the evil within women. According to one tradition, *ANGRA MAINYU*, the principle or spirit of darkness, kissed Jahi and thus introduced the impurity of menstruation to women.

DUMUZI was the husband of *INANA*, the goddess of love and queen of heaven. He is the Sumerian equivalent of the Babylonian god *TAMMUZ*. In the Babylonian version of the goddess's journey to the underworld, *ISHTAR* descended into *ERESHKIGAL*'s kingdom in order to rescue Tammuz and awaken him from his sleep. However, in the Sumerian version of the myth, Dumuzi was seized by the demons of the underworld as a substitute for Inana on the goddess's own orders.

When Inana returned from the underworld to her city of Uruk, to find Dumuzi sitting happily on a throne rather than mourning her, she fastened the eye of death on him and elected that he should go to the underworld in her place. Dumuzi prayed to the sun god for help. The sun god turned Dumuzi into a snake and he escaped.

Dumuzi told his sister, Geshtinanna, about a dream in which he saw his own death, and Geshtinanna was overcome with grief. When the demons approached once more, Dumuzi changed into a gazelle. However, the demons found Dumuzi and again attacked him. This time, they succeed in dragging him away.

Dumuzi was mourned by Inana, his mother, and his sister Geshtinanna. Inana was so moved by Geshtinanna's grief that she eventually agreed that her husband need spend only half of each year in the underworld, with Geshtinanna taking his place for the other half.

EA, the Babylonian god of the earth, was tempted in a story reminiscent of that of Adam and Eve. (ILLUSTRATION FROM MYTHS OF BABYLONIA AND ASSYRIA BY DONALD A MACKENZIE.)

EA, or Enki, a Babylonian deity, was one of a trinity of creator gods that also included the sky god *ANU* and the wind god *ENLIL*. He corresponds to the Sumerian god Enki. *EA* lived in *APSU*, the primordial ocean that surrounded and supported the earth. He was the son of *ANSHAR* and Kishar, the male and female principles.

A god of the fresh waters, as well as of wisdom and magic, Ea had the power of an oracle and would advise and reason with human beings. When Apsu was plotting the destruction of the gods, Ea killed him, prompting *TIAMAT*'s fury. Later, when the god Enlil decided to destroy humanity, the wise Ea warned humankind of the conspiracy and advised Enlil to

EA was a Babylonian god who helped people survive by teaching them how to plough and till the land. With the sky god Anu and the wind god Enlil, he formed a trinity of creator gods. (BABYLONIAN SEAL.)

temper his fury. On earth, Ea lived in the city of Eridu, on the southern edge of Sumer. His home was the Ezuab or "House of the Apsu". Ea is usually represented as a goat with a fish's tail or as part human, part fish. His consort was Ninki, the "Lady of the Earth", or sometimes Damkina or Damgalnunna.

Ea was introduced into the Hittite pantheon by the Hurrians. In the story of the weather god *TESHUB*'s battle with *ULLIKUMMI*, Teshub seeks advice from Ea the wise. The gods are dismayed at Ullikummi's power, but Ea decides to visit Upelluri, on whose shoulder Ullikummi had been raised. Upelluri says, "When heaven and earth were built upon me I knew nothing of it, and when they came and cut heaven and earth asunder with a cutting tool, that also I knew not. Now something is hurting my right shoulder, but I know not who that god is." The god was Ullikummi, who was made of diorite stone. Ea used the ancient saw that had been used to separate heaven from earth to cut the stone creature's feet, thereby destroying Ullikummi's power.

MYTHS OF THE FLOOD

A LIMITLESS OCEAN FEATURED IN MANY creation myths as the primeval state of the world. A flood of global proportions was also a common theme, in which an inundation was sent to wipe out sinful humankind and thus restore the world to its pristine original state, so that it could be repopulated by a nobler race. The Egyptians believed that their creator god, Ra, would one day tire of humanity and return the world to the watery abyss of Nun before beginning a new cycle of creation. Stories of overwhelming floods reflected the ambiguous nature of humanity's relationship with water, which was vital to life but also carried the threat of violence and devastation. The Tigris and Euphrates, the two rivers on which the

civilizations of Mesopotamia depended, flooded unpredictably, and their fearsome nature is expressed in several versions of the flood myth, which was to find its way into the Hebraic tradition as the familiar story of Noah's ark.

ENLIL (above), as Sumerian god of the air, controlled the terrifying forces of nature. Angered by the noise rising from overpopulated cities, he determined to destroy the inhabitants of the earth, and sent a flood so great that even the other gods were frightened. Warned by the water god, Ea, the wise man Utnapishtim weathered the cataclysm in his boat and was rewarded by Enlil with the gift of eternal life.
(*ILLUSTRATION BY E. WALLCOUSINS FROM MYTHS OF BABYLONIA AND ASSYRIA BY DONALD MACKENZIE.*)

NOAH (left) and his family were the only human survivors of the flood that covered the earth for 150 days before its level began to fall, and it deposited Noah's ark on Mount Ararat. Noah released a dove who failed to find dry land and came back to take refuge on the ark. Seven days later he released her again, and this time, though she was forced to return, she carried an olive branch as a sign that the flood was abating at last.
(*CATALAN BOOK ILLUSTRATION, C. AD 970.*)

NOAH (above) released his dove a third time, seven days after her return carrying the olive branch. This time, she left the ark for good. Noah, looking out, saw dry land once more and was able to disembark. God promised him and his family that they were safe, and as a token of his covenant, he set a rainbow in the sky, which would appear when rainclouds threatened as reassurance that the flood would not return. (THE DOVE SENT FORTH FROM THE ARK BY GUSTAVE DORÉ, 19TH CENTURY.)

NOAH (above right) was given a precise specification for the ark by God, detailing the dimensions of the boat, its roof and door, the number of decks, the type of wood to use and how it should be waterproofed. Noah was already an extremely old man at the time of the flood and lived on for many more years after it – his longevity recalls the eternal life granted to the survivors in the Mesopotamian versions of the myth. (DETAIL OF THE VERDUN ALTAR, 1181.)

UTNAPISHTIM's (right) boat eventually came to rest on Mount Nisir and, as the water began to subside, he sent out a dove and a swallow. Both returned to the boat unable to find food or a place to perch. However, when a raven was released, it did not come back, and Utnapishtim concluded that it had found dry land. He offered a sacrifice on the summit of the mountain, which placated the gods. (ILLUSTRATION FROM GILGAMESH BY ZABELLE C BOYAJIAN, 1924.)

EL, a Canaanite deity, was referred to as the "Father of the Gods". He caused the rivers to flow, thus making the land fertile, and made his home near the seashore. Sometimes referred to as "Creator of the Earth", he was also known as "Bull", or "Bull-El", to signify his strength and powers of fertility. His name is usually translated as "Mighty One" or "First One". In 1929, stories about El were found on clay tablets at Ras Shamra in Syria, the site of the ancient city of Ugarit. The tablets dated from the 14th century BC.

Although El was usually regarded as the consort of Asherat (see ASTARTE), one myth found at Ras Shamra tells how he had intercourse with two women, probably representing Asherat and ANAT. The women subsequently gave birth to the deities SHACHAR, "Dawn", and SHALIM, "Dusk". According to the story recorded on the clay tablets, El walked along the shore, then plunged into the waves. His hands reached out like the waves, and he made his wives fruitful. He kissed their lips, which tasted as sweet as grapes, and in the kiss, and the conception and the embrace, Dawn and Dusk were

EL, the creator god, sits on his throne and listens to the prayer of a supplicant. (RELIEF ON A STELE, SYRIA, 13TH CENTURY BC.)

born. El went on to father many more deities. He was depicted as an old man, sitting on a throne and wearing bull's horns.

EL-'OZZA see AL-UZZA.

ENKI see EA.

ENLIL was originally worshipped in Sumer as "Lord of the Wind", the god of hurricanes who represented the power of nature. He was believed to have absolute power over humans and was represented among men by the earthly kings.

Long before humankind was created, Enlil was said to have supervised the gods in their task of digging out the beds of the Tigris and Euphrates rivers. In time, the gods became exhausted by their ceaseless toil and decided to rebel. Enlil was devastated, but the god Enki (see EA) came to his aid, suggesting that the goddess Nintur create humankind in order to take over the work from the gods. For hundreds of years, all went smoothly, but then the cities

became so overpopulated that the clamour made by the men and women kept Enlil awake. Enlil decided to solve the problem by sending a plague down to earth. However, Enki warned the people of the impending disaster, and they made huge efforts to keep quiet.

In time, the men and women forgot Enlil's threat and reverted to their noisy ways. This time, Enlil threatened to send a drought down to earth. Once again, Enki warned the people and they became quiet. The next time that Enlil was disturbed by the people's clamour, the god threatened to instigate a famine, but again Enki warned humankind and they were quiet.

Finally, when the men and women again began to create a huge clamour, Enlil lost all patience and sent down a massive flood. However, Enki had advised a wise man to build a ship and to save himself and his family from the flood. In some versions of the myth, the wise man was called Atrahasis, in others, Ziusadra. For seven days and seven nights, the rains lashed down, and the world was submerged by a massive flood. When the waters finally subsided, only Atrahasis (or Ziusadra), his

ENLIL, Sumerian "Lord of the Wind", receives worshippers at his throne. Son of the sky god, Anu, he represented the power of nature and threatened to destroy humankind because the clamour they made kept him awake. (CYLINDER SEAL, MESOPOTAMIAN, 3RD MILLENNIUM BC.)

family and the animals on the boat remained alive. In another version of the flood myth, which forms part of the epic of GILGAMESH, the hero UTNAPISHTIM survives the flood with his family.

In earliest times, Enlil's consort was believed to be NINHURSAGA, the "Lady of the Great Mountain". Later, however, he was associated with the grain goddess, NINLIL.

The Babylonians often equated Enlil with the great god MARDUK, calling him Bel, or "Lord". He was also assimilated into the Hittite pantheon, by way of the Hurrians. There, he features in the myth of the monstrous being ULLIKUMMI. (See also MYTHS OF THE FLOOD)

ENNUGI see UTNAPISHTIM.

ERESHKIGAL was the queen of the underworld in both Akkadian and Babylonian mythology. The underworld lay beneath the waters of APSU, the primordial ocean. It was a dry and dark realm, sometimes referred to as a mountain, sometimes as enemy territory. According to the epic of GILGAMESH, Ereshkigal, rather than having chosen her kingdom, was "given the underworld for her domain." Enthroned therein, she ate only clay and drank dirty water.

The goddess had an insatiable sexual appetite and never let compassion for others stand in the way of her desires. According to one story, when the war god Nergal entered the underworld, Ereshkigal

EVE was created by God, who placed her in paradise as a companion for Adam. (NUREMBERG BIBLE, 1483.)

copulated with him for six days and nights. None the less, when he left, she remained unsatisfied.

In order that no one should return to the land of the living, the underworld was guarded by seven walls. At each of its seven gates, people had to take off an item of clothing, each representing one of their earthly attributes. When they finally reached the centre, they found themselves naked and imprisoned forever in eternal darkness. According to one tradition, Ereshkigal was the sole ruler of the underworld until Nergal invaded her territory, posting two demons at each gate. In order to achieve peace, Ereshkigal agreed to marry Nergal and to give him authority over the underworld. Ereshkigal was the sister of the fertility goddess ISHTAR, the counterpart of the Sumerian goddess INANA.

ETANA was the 12th king of the city state of Kish after the flood. King Etana grew miserable because he had no children and appealed to the sun god SHAMASH for help. Shamash told Etana to go to a particular mountain. There, on the mountain, an eagle and a serpent had recently had a terrible quarrel. Each of the creatures had children but the eagle had eaten all the serpent's offspring. The serpent

complained to Shamash, who told him to trap the eagle and leave him to die. Etana found the dying eagle and asked him for a special herb that would enable him to have a son. The eagle promised Etana that he would bring him the herb if he would cure him. For several months, Etana brought the eagle food and drink until finally the bird was fully recovered. Then, the eagle told Etana to sit on his back so that he could carry him up to the sky of ANU, the supreme god. The eagle flew up to the gods and continued flying upwards towards the dwelling place of ISHTAR, the fertility goddess. In some versions of the tale, Etana seems to succeed in his quest and is given the herb by Ishtar. In another version, Etana grows dizzy and begs the eagle to return to earth. However, the eagle's strength suddenly runs out, and the two of them fall to the ground with a mighty crash.

EVE was the first woman, according to the Hebrew creation story. She was said to have been formed from her husband ADAM's rib. A serpent tempted Eve to eat the one fruit which God had forbidden the couple, and she persuaded Adam to join her. As a result, both Adam and Eve were expelled from paradise. Eve was seen as responsible for the Fall and for bringing death, sin and sorrow into the world.

Christians have often viewed Eve's sin as a sexual failing. However, the Fall also opened the way for growth and learning. Adam refers to Eve as Hawwah, which is usually translated as "Mother of All Living", or "She who gives Life". According to one tradition, Adam was buried in paradise and was promised resurrection, whereas Eve was buried with her son, Abel. (See also SERPENTS AND DRAGONS)

EVE bears the apple, traditionally the forbidden fruit that led to the Fall and expulsion from paradise. (EVE BY LUCAS CRANACH THE ELDER, OIL ON WOOD, C. 1528.)

G

EYE see *HATHOR*.

FATIMA, the prophet Muhammad's daughter, is regarded by Isma'ilis as the "Mother of the Holy Imams". The Imams are the semi-divine leaders of Shi'ism, one of the two great forms of Islam of which the Isma'ilis form a subsect. Fatima is revered within esoteric Islam and is seen as symbolizing the "supra-celestial earth". She is considered to be the source of the Imams' wisdom because she is the "hidden tablet; upon which God has written."

FERIDUN, according to ancient Iranian mythology, was the hero destined to overthrow *ZOHAK*, the evil king sometimes regarded as the embodiment of the terrifying monster *AZHI DAHAKA*.

Zohak was warned in a dream that he would be deposed by someone called Feridun, and consequently ordered the massacre of all children. However, Feridun's mother, Firanak, saved her baby by hiding him in a garden, where he was suckled by a miraculous cow called Purmajeh. Firanak then hid the baby in Hindustan.

Throughout Feridun's childhood years, Zohak was obsessed with the thought that his destroyer was alive somewhere. Sure enough, Feridun grew up determined to overthrow the evil king.

One day, a man whose children had been killed by Zohak led a group of rebels to Feridun's palace. Feridun decided that the time was ripe for action. As he marched towards the king, an angel taught him magic and comforted him with tales of his future happiness. Zohak, learning of Feridun's approach, clad himself in armour. He attacked Feridun with his sword, whereupon Feridun smashed it with a club. However, an angel told Feridun not to kill the king but to chain him in a cave under a mountain. Feridun did as he was told and then succeeded to

FATIMA, daughter of the prophet Muhammad, on her way to a Jewish wedding party with Muhammad, A'isha, Umm Salma and Umm al-Ayman, receives a gift of a green cloak brought by Gabriel from paradise.

the throne. His reign lasted for several hundred years. (See also *SERPENTS AND DRAGONS*)

THE FRAVASHIS, according to the mythology of ancient Iran, were benevolent spirits or guardian angels. They helped *AHURA MAZDA* to create the world, and defended heaven from its enemies with their sharp spears while riding their fleet-

GEB, the Egyptian god of the earth, was the brother and consort of the sky goddess, Nut. (PAPYRUS.)

footed steeds. They were believed to be the ancestral spirits of believers, a part of the human soul that Ahura Mazda had created before each individual's birth, and thus might be regarded as prototypes for living beings. Fravashi is usually translated as "She who is Chosen".

GABRIEL, or Jibril, is known as the spirit of truth or "Angel of Revelations" in Islamic tradition. He stands at the apex of the angelic host and is said to have dictated the Qur'an to Muhammad. Gabriel is also believed to stand at the north-east corner of the *KA'ABA*, Islam's most sacred shrine.

In the Bible, Gabriel appears as the messenger of *YAHWEH*. He visited the Old Testament patriarch *DANIEL* twice, to announce the return of the Hebrews from captivity in Babylon and to explain the diversity of nations. In the New Testament, it is the archangel Gabriel who brings Mary the tidings that she is to conceive Jesus. Gabriel is also the trumpeter who will sound the Last Judgment. According to Hebrew apocalyptic literature, Gabriel is an angel of retribution and death. (See also *ANGELS AND DJINN*)

GADD was the name given to a variety of beneficent deities in pre-Islamic northern Arabia. It is sometimes believed to refer merely to a personification of good luck.

GAYOMART was the primeval being of ancient Iranian mythology. His corpse, together with that of the primeval bull *GEUSH URVAN*, was said to have given rise to all life. According to tradition, Gayomart existed for 3,000 years as a spirit until, in the second great epoch, he was made into a physical being by *AHURA MAZDA*, the principle of

GABRIEL, angel of the Annunciation, tells Mary that she is to conceive Jesus. He is also believed to stand at the Ka'aba, Islam's most sacred shrine, containing the Black Stone. (ICON, 12TH CENTURY.)

goodness. He was killed by *ANGRA MAINYU*, the principle of darkness. According to one myth, all the parts of the universe were created from his body; another tale tells how the seed of Gayomart was buried in the ground for 40 years, until it gave rise to the first human couple, *MASHYA AND MASHYOI*, as well as the seven metals. Gayomart's name is translated as "Mortal Life", or "Dying Life".

GEB, the Egyptian god of the earth, was the brother and consort of *NUT*, and the eldest son of *SHU* and Tefnut, the deities of air and moisture. Shu, or in some stories *RA*, was said to have separated Geb and Nut from a passionate embrace by violently pushing them apart so that Nut formed the sky and Geb the earth. Until then, there had not been sufficient space between the two bodies for Nut to give birth. Geb was said to grieve continuously for having been parted from his beloved Nut, and his distress was said to cause earthquakes.

He was usually regarded as a beneficent deity who provided humanity with crops for their fields, and who healed the sick. However, it was also feared that he might trap the dead within his body and thereby prevent them from entering the underworld. The god was usually depicted as a bearded man, often lying under the feet of Shu. He was sometimes coloured green, to indicate that vegetation was believed to grow from his body. Occasionally he was accompanied by a goose or portrayed as a bull.

Geb, the "Father of the Gods", and Nut were said to have begat *OSIRIS, ISIS, NEPHTHYS* and *SETH*. The kings of Egypt called themselves the "Heirs of Geb".

GEUSH URVAN, the primeval bull of ancient Iranian mythology, was created, along with the primeval man *GAYOMART*, by *AHURA MAZDA*, the essence of good. According to one tradition, Geush Urvan died, like Gayomart, at the hands of *ANGRA MAINYU*, the essence of darkness. Another tradition teaches that Geush Urvan was slain by *MITHRA*. All kinds of plants and animals were said to emerge from his corpse.

Widely believed to be the guardian of cattle, Geush Urvan's name means "Soul of the Cow". The sacrifice of a bull was an important part of Mithraic rituals.

GILGAMESH, the famous Mesopotamian hero, is believed to be based on a real person, who was most probably a Sumerian king. *The Epic of Gilgamesh*, a poem recording the hero's exploits, was transcribed on to tablets in the second millennium BC.

Gilgamesh was two-thirds god, one-third man. He was so active and such a womanizer that the inhabitants of Uruk, or Erech, the city where he lived, appealed to the gods for help. The deities responded by creating another man called Enkidu, or Eabani, who turned out to be a wild and savage being, even more troublesome than Gilgamesh. Eventually, it was Gilgamesh who helped the people of Uruk to hatch a plot whereby they succeeded in taming the wild being. Enkidu subsequently became Gilgamesh's friend and constant companion, and the two men lived a life of luxury together.

In time, however, Gilgamesh was instructed by the gods to leave his home in order to fight Khumbaba, or Huwawa, the horrible monster who lived some 20,000 marching hours away from Uruk at Cedar Mountain. Enkidu and Gilgamesh set off on their quest and, after entering the cedar forest, eventually found Khumbaba's home. Gilgamesh

challenged the monster to battle and, after a fearsome struggle, the two men overcame him, although it was Enkidu's spear that struck the fatal blow.

Soon afterwards, the goddess *INANA* tried to seduce Gilgamesh. When the hero turned her down, she complained to the god An (see *ANU*) who was eventually persuaded to give Inana the bull of heaven to send against Gilgamesh. However, Enkidu caught the bull and Gilgamesh stabbed it to death. The gods, outraged that the bull had been killed, took their revenge by striking Enkidu down with illness. After a few days, he died.

Gilgamesh was devastated at the death of his friend, and became terrified at the thought of death. He decided to try and discover the secret of immortality and set out on a quest to find *UTNAPISHTIM*, the hero who, after surviving the flood, had been granted immortality by the gods. When he reached Mount Mashu, Gilgamesh was confronted by the scorpion men who guarded its gates. However, they recognized that he was in part divine and let him pass by them to proceed into the mountain.

At length, Gilgamesh came to a beautiful garden beside a sea and saw before him the tree of the gods,

laden with amazing fruits, the ground covered with jewels. There, he met the goddess Siduri Sabitu, who tried to deter the hero from his quest. At Gilgamesh's insistence, the goddess eventually advised him to seek the help of Ushanabi, Utnapishtim's boatman. Ushanabi took Gilgamesh through the waters of death into the underworld, and at last, the hero reached Utnapishtim. Gilgamesh told him: "Because of my brother I am afraid of death; because of my brother I stray through the wilderness. His fate lies heavy upon me. How can I be silent, how can I rest? He is dust, and I shall die also and be laid in the earth for ever." The hero of the flood told Gilgamesh that death, like sleep, was necessary for humankind. To prove his point, he told Gilgamesh to try staying awake for six days and seven nights. Gilgamesh agreed, but fell fast asleep almost as soon as he had sat down.

Before Gilgamesh returned home, Utnapishtim showed him the plant of youth, which lay at the bottom of the ocean. Gilgamesh found the plant, but as he bent to pick it, it was stolen by a snake. The tale ends on a sad note, with the ghost of Enkidu telling Gilgamesh of the misery of life in the underworld. (See also *UNDER-WORLDS; HEROES AND QUESTS*)

GUBABA see *KUBABA*.

GULA see *NINURTA*.

GULASES see *GULSES*.

THE GULSES, or Gulases, were Hittite goddesses whose name means either "Scribes", or "Female Determiners of Fate". The Gulses allotted the destinies of individual

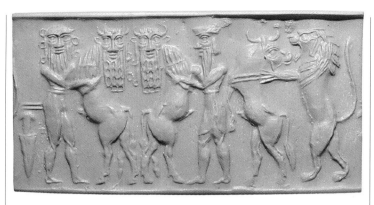

men and women, dispensing good and evil as well as life and death. The Hurrians called them Hutena.

HADAD see *BAAL*.

THE HAFAZA, according to Islamic mythology, are a type of guardian spirit. They look after people, protecting them from *DJINN*, or demons. Everybody is said to be protected by four hafaza: two to watch over them during the day and two during the night. The hafaza record each individual's good and bad deeds. People are said to be most at risk from the djinn at sunset and at dawn since, at those times, the hafaza are changing guard.

HAHHIMAS, the disappearing god, according to one version of the Hittite myth of *TELEPINU*, was responsible for having caused the great devastation that afflicted the earth. The myth tells how "Hahhimas has paralysed the whole earth, he has dried up the waters, Hahhimas is mighty!" In response to this desperate state of affairs, the weather god *TARU* called on his brother, the wind, to breathe on the earth, thereby reinvigorating it. However, on his return, the wind simply reported that the whole earth was paralysed and that people were doing nothing but eating and drinking. Hahhimas then began to seize and paralyse the gods, including Telepinu. Hahhimas's name is sometimes translated as "Torpor".

HAN-UZZAI see *AL-UZZA*.

HANNAHANNA was the Hittite mother goddess and goddess of birth. Her name is usually translated as "Grandmother". She was served by the bee who eventually found the fertility god *TELEPINU* after he had disappeared from the world, leaving decay and death behind him. *TESHUB* protested at the bee being sent on the mission, saying, "The gods great and small have sought him but have not found him. Shall this bee now search and find him?" However, Hannahanna ignored Teshub's objections and told the bee to bring Telepinu home.

The bee searched the earth, and eventually found Telepinu asleep in a field. As directed by Hannahanna, the insect stung the god. Enraged, Telepinu embarked on a bout of destruction, killing humans and animals. The story may be influenced by the belief that honey has the power to expel evil spirits.

HAOMA, according to ancient Iranian mythology, was the lord of all medicinal plants. He was able to confer immortality on his followers and was sometimes said to be the son of *AHURA MAZDA*, the supreme god and principle of good. Equivalent to the Indian Soma, haoma was also a real herb from which an intoxicating drink could be made. The drink was believed to heighten spiritual awareness and also to confer immortality. It was used in sacrificial rituals, which

GILGAMESH and his friend Enkidu fought bulls during their quest together, which culminated in the death of the monster Khumbaba. (AKKADIAN CYLINDER SEAL IMPRESSION, 3RD MILLENNIUM BC.)

were said to drive away evil spirits. The spirit of the great religious reformer *ZOROASTER* was said to be strengthened by drinking haoma.

HAOSHYANGHA, or Hoshang or Husheng, the son of Siyamek, was the first king, according to ancient Iranian mythology. Siyamek, the son of *MASHYA AND MASHYOI*, the first human couple, was killed by a demon. After killing the demon, Haoshyangha spread peace throughout his kingdom and then proceeded to spread justice throughout the world. He introduced all the arts of civilization to human beings. After extracting iron from a stone, he taught humankind how to make axes, saws and hoes. He then organized a system of irrigation, leading water from the rivers to the fields, and tamed wild animals so that they could be used to cultivate the land. He also taught people to make clothing from the skins of wild animals.

HAPI see *APIS*.

HARSIESIS see *HORUS*.

HAOMA was both a god of medicine and the name of a magical herb. Zoroaster was said to have drunk a fortifying potion made from haoma. (LIEBIG "CHROMO" CARD, 19TH CENTURY.)

HATHOR (above), was depicted as a cow, or as a woman wearing a horned headdress with a solar disc. (TEMPLE OF HUREMHEB, EGYPT.)

HATHOR (left), daughter of the god Ra, in her usual form of a cow. She nourished the living with her milk and carried the dead to the underworld. (TEMPLE OF HATSHEPSUT, EGYPT.)

HATHOR, the Egyptian sky goddess and daughter of the sun god, RA, was usually represented as a cow. The goddess of joy and love, dance and song, she looked after mothers and children. She nurtured the living and carried the dead to the underworld. There, she refreshed them with food and drink from the sycamore tree, in which it was believed she was incarnated. Royal coffins were made from sycamore trees, in the belief or hope that death was no more than a return to the womb.

HATHOR, as the goddess Sekhmet, is depicted in human form, with the head of a lioness surmounted by a sun disc, identifying her as the daughter of Ra.

The Eye of Ra was identified with Hathor. When Ra grew old, humankind began to plot against him. Hearing of this, the enraged god decided to send the divine Eye, the terrifying, burning power of the sun, to slaughter them. The Eye took the form of Hathor who, as the lioness Sekhmet, or the "Powerful One", threw herself at all the wicked men and women and killed them in a massive bloodbath. Eventually, Ra decided that enough carnage had been inflicted, and he called an end to the slaughter. Only by Ra's intervention was Sekhmet prevented from destroying humanity.

In order to put an end to Sekhmet's relentless slaughter, Ra drenched the battleground in thousands of jugs of beer mixed with pomegranate juice. The blood-thirsty Sekhmet drank the bright red potion, believing it was blood, and became so inebriated that she ceased her attack and was transformed back into the beautiful Hathor. In remembrance of the event, great jugs of beer and pomegranate juice were drunk annually on Hathor's feast day. (See also SACRED ANIMALS)

HAZZI was a mountain god worshipped by both the Hurrians and the Hittites. He formed part of the retinue of the weather god, TARU, and was invoked at Hittite state occasions as a god of oaths. Hazzi was also the home of the gods; it is thought to have been situated on Mount Sapon, near Ugarit.

HEBAT see HEPAT.

HEPAT, or Hebat or Hepit, the chief goddess of the Hurrians, was sometimes referred to as the "Queen of Heaven". The wife of the tempest god TESHUB, she was often granted almost equal status with her husband, and occasionally took precedence over him. She and Teshub produced a son, Sharruma, who was represented as a pair of human legs. When Hepat heard that ULLIKUMMI had forced Teshub to abdicate, she nearly fell off the roof of a tower in horror: "If she had made a single step she would have fallen from the roof, but her women held her and did not let her fall." Hepat was assimilated into the Hittite pantheon, where she was often equated with ARINNA, the sun goddess. She was depicted either sitting on a throne or standing on a lion, her sacred animal.

HEPIT see HEPAT.

HERARHTY see HORUS.

HORUS, in the story of ISIS and OSIRIS, is sometimes known as Harsiesis to distinguish him from the twenty or so other Horuses in the Egyptian pantheon. He was depicted as a falcon or with a falcon's head. He was born, after Osiris had retired to the underworld, on the island of Chemmis near Bhutto and was raised there in secret by Isis. Harsiesis eventually avenged Osiris's death at the hands of SETH, and reclaimed the throne. He ruled peacefully, and was worshipped throughout Egypt.

Horus was worshipped as the god of the sky. His eyes were said to be the sun and moon.

Herakhty, or "Horus of the Horizon", was a sun god who rose each morning on the eastern horizon. He was often identified with the sun god, RA, and was eventually absorbed by him, forming Ra-Herakhty.

HOSHANG see HAOSHYANGHA.

HORUS (above) was the son of Osiris and Isis, and a cosmic deity. He was depicted as a falcon or with a falcon's head. As the first ruler of all Egypt, he wore the double crown of the united kingdom. (RELIEF OF THE TEMPLE OF SETI I IN HYPOSTYLE, 1303–1290 BC.)

HORUS (left) in battle. Raised in secret by his mother, Isis, he eventually avenged his father Osiris's death at the hands of Seth and reclaimed the throne.

HOURIS, in Islamic mythology, were black-eyed women who provided dead men in paradise with sexual pleasure. Each man was said to be given 72 houris, whose virginity was eternally renewed.

HUBAL was a god worshipped in Arabia in pre-Islamic times. His image, made from red carnelian, still stands in the sacred KA'ABA in Mecca, Islam's holiest city. It is believed that the Black Stone of the Ka'aba might be connected with the god in some way. Hubal was particularly famed for his oracle.

HUPASIYAS was the lover of INARAS, the Hittite goddess whose duties seem to have been those of protecting gods and tradesmen. A mortal being, Hupasiyas bound the monstrous dragon or snake ILLUYANKAS with a rope after Inaras had trapped the creature at a feast. The weather god TARU then killed Illuyankas. Inaras rewarded Hupasiyas for his help by building him a house. She warned him that he must never look out of the windows of his new home in case he saw his mortal wife and children. When Hupasiyas disobeyed the goddess, she killed him.

HUSHEDAR, according to ancient Iranian mythology, is a saviour and a son of the prophet ZOROASTER. Hushedar would be succeeded every thousand years by other saviours, culminating in SAOSHYANT, who is expected to introduce the universal judgment of humankind.

Eventually, after a final conflict between good and evil, the universe will be made pure again, and humanity will dwell in perfection with AHURA MAZDA.

HUSHENG see HAOSHYANGHA.

HUTENA see GULSES.

IBLIS is the name for the devil in Islamic belief. He is a rebel against God and tempts humankind to evil. Originally, he was the angel Arazil. When ALLAH created the first man, ADAM, out of clay, Arazil refused to worship him. When Allah summoned the angels to praise his creation, Arazil refused to attend. As a result, Arazil was thrown out of paradise, and from then onwards he encouraged the DJINN to make war against Allah. Eventually, he brought about Adam and Eve's fall from grace by tempting them into sin.

On the Day of Judgment, Iblis and his hosts of evil spirits will be consigned to the fires of hell. It is disputed whether Iblis was an angel or a djinn since, though he behaved like a fallen angel, he was said to have been made from smokeless fire like a djinn.

SERPENTS AND DRAGONS

HUMAN FEARS OF POWERFUL, ungovernable forces were crystallized in visions of huge and terrifying monsters. Serpents and dragons were composite images of everything that was inhuman: scales, claws and wings, of fantastic, fearful strength and size. They might also exhibit the characteristics of other animals, such as the head of a lion and the talons of an eagle. Their hybrid appearance added to their monstrous nature. Many were sea creatures, embodying the malign power of unpredictable nature and the threat of chaos. The most dramatic myths

concern human or immortal heroes who killed dragons that threatened the world. By destroying the monsters, heroes were able to restore order and preserve the safety of civilization. As emblems of chaos, serpents featured in creation stories such as the myth of the snake Apep, coiled in the primeval water, who fertilized the cosmic egg of the Egyptians. In time, snakes came to represent not just disorder, but evil.

THE SERPENT (above) in the Garden of Eden is frequently portrayed with the face of Lilith, who in Hebrew legend was Adam's first wife. She considered herself his equal and left him – and Eden – rather than submit to him. She was often depicted as winged, with the body of a snake, and was said to be the temptress of Eve. She acquired the character of a wicked demon who killed new-born babies and was the enemy of men. (ANONYMOUS ENGRAVING.)

EVE (left), with her partner Adam, was free to eat the fruit of every tree in the Garden of Eden except one, the tree of the knowledge of good and evil. The serpent, more subtle than any other beast, persuaded Eve that this was the one fruit she desired and, having tasted it, Eve gave it to Adam to eat. According to the Old Testament of the Bible, their disobedience condemned humans to lives of toil, hardship and death. The serpent's punishment was to crawl on its belly and eat dust, and to be the enemy of humankind thereafter. (ILLUSTRATION BY RICHARD RIEMERSCHMID.)

LEVIATHAN (left), the great sea monster, was said to have existed from the fifth day of creation, and to represent the forces of chaos subordinated by Yahweh. According to later Hebrew traditions, Leviathan will be vanquished in a great final battle with the archangel Gabriel, and the banquet celebrating the eventual arrival of the Messiah will take place in a tent made from the monster's skin. (LEVIATHAN BY ARTHUR RACKHAM, 1908.)

AARON'S ROD (above), was turned into a serpent by Yahweh to help Moses and Aaron persuade the pharoah to allow the Israelites to leave Egypt. The pharaoh sent for all the sorcerers and magicians of Egypt, who responded by miraculously turning their own staffs into serpents as well, but they were all eaten by Aaron's. (AND HE THREW DOWN HIS ROD. . ., BY QAJAR, miniature, c. 1860–70.)

APEP (left) the great serpent, lay in wait in the Egyptian underworld to ambush the sun god, who had to voyage through it each night ready to rise again. Night was a time of uncertainty and danger for the god, as it was for humans on earth. The return of the sun in the morning represented the triumph of life over death, symbolized by Ra-Herakhty, the falcon, vanquishing the serpent. (SMALL LIMESTONE PYRAMID.)

MARDUK's (above) battle with Tiamat is part of the Babylonian creation myth. Tiamat was the primeval salt-water ocean, which had to be tamed to allow the universe to come into existence. Marduk subdued her and eventually split her in two to create the earth and sky. Her eyes became the sources of the rivers Tigris and Euphrates. Marduk went on to kill her son, Kingu, and mixed his blood with earth to create humankind. (ILLUSTRATION FROM GILGAMESH BY ZABELLE C BOYAJIAN, 1924.)

DRAGONS (right) were appropriate emblems for the stars mapped by Arabic astronomers. These cosmic creatures engaged in battles far beyond human realms, such as the encounter between the Persian hero Feridun and the mighty dragon Azhi Dahaka. When Feridun stabbed the monster, snakes, toads and scorpions began to pour out, so instead of cutting him up, the hero imprisoned him in Mount Demavend. (ILLUSTRATION FROM A DESCRIPTION OF THE FIXED STARS, 1629.)

IBRAHIM see *ABRAHAM*.

ILLUYANKAS was the monstrous snake or dragon of Hittite mythology. He waged war against the gods, particularly against the weather god, *TARU*. However, the monster was eventually slain by Taru, who was assisted in his assault by the goddess *INARAS* and her mortal lover, *HUPASIYAS*. In another version of the tale, Illuyankas seized the heart and eyes of the weather god. Taru responded by fathering a son whom he married to the daughter of Illuyankas, demanding the missing organs as a dowry payment. Taru then succeeded in slaying the monster.

The story of Illuyankas and Taru was assimilated into Canaanite mythology as the struggle of the gods against the *LEVIATHAN*. The Hittite monster was also the prototype for Typhon, the hundred-headed beast of Greek mythology. The tale of Taru's battle against Illuyankas was recited at an annual feast either of the New Year or of spring. The destruction of the monster was believed to signal the beginning of a new era.

IMHOTEP was a sage and scholar attached to the court of the ancient King Zoser, who ruled Egypt in the third millennium BC. A great architect, as well as an astronomer and scientist, Imhotep designed and oversaw the construction of the first pyramids. Until then, rulers had been buried in underground chambers. Imhotep's Step Pyramid at Saqqara was the first monumental stone building ever constructed. The sage was also credited with ending a seven-year famine by advising the king to make offerings to *KHNUM*, the god who controlled the flood waters of the Nile.

Admired during his lifetime, Imhotep gradually came to be celebrated as a god. According to some tales, he was the son of the great god *PTAH* and provided the high priest of Ptah with a son. The patron of scribes, he is usually depicted as a priest with a shaven head. He was also the patron of doctors. His name means "He Who Comes in Peace." (See also *GATEWAYS TO THE GODS*)

INANA, the goddess of love, fertility and war, queen of heaven and earth, was the most important goddess in the Sumerian pantheon. Her symbol was the reed bundle, and she was often portrayed with bright sunbeams radiating from her image. Inana's Babylonian equivalent was the goddess *ISHTAR*.

Like Ishtar, Inana descended to the underworld kingdom of *ERESHKIGAL*. At the gate, Inana explained why she had come: "Because of my sister Ereshkigal". Then, however, she claimed that she wanted to see the funeral of Gugalanna, the "Bull of Heaven".

IMHOTEP, studying a papyrus. Probable architect of the famous Step Pyramid at Saqqara, and greatly admired during his lifetime, Imhotep gradually came to be celebrated as one of the gods.

INANA with Ea and Gilgamesh. She was the most important goddess in the Sumerian pantheon. (AKKADIAN CYLINDER SEAL, 3RD MILLENNIUM BC.)

At each of the gates of the underworld, Inana divested herself of one of her items of clothing, or earthly attributes, including her priestly office, her sexual powers and her royal powers. Finally, she was condemned to death and killed, becoming part of the underworld kingdom.

The goddess Ninshubur, Inana's handmaiden, mourned grievously for her queen and eventually appealed to the gods for help. Neither *ENLIL* nor Nanna (see *SIN*) would become involved. However, the god *EA* came to Inana's aid. From the dirt of his fingernails, he created two beings who, because they were sexless, were able to enter the land of infertility. These beings were mourners who eased the ceaseless pain of Ereshkigal, whose existence had been one of continuous rejection. In reward for thus soothing the ruler of the underworld, the beings asked that they be allowed to revive Inana. Ereshkigal agreed and the goddess was reborn.

Before leaving, Inana had to agree to find someone to take her place in the underworld. The goddess was escorted on her homeward journey by a group of horrific demons.

When she reached the world of the living, Inana found her handmaiden, Ninshubur, waiting for her by the gates of the underworld and her two sons waiting for her in their temples. All three were in mourning. However, she was aghast to discover that her husband *DUMUZI*, far from mourning her death, was thoroughly enjoying himself. Not only was he seated on his throne but he was also dressed in the splendid garments which she herself had given him. Furious with rage, Inana immediately appointed Dumuzi as her substitute in the underworld.

Although Dumuzi attempted to hide, he was eventually dragged off by the demons who had accompanied Inana on her homeward journey. Geshtinanna, Dumuzi's sister, was so distraught that she offered to share Dumuzi's sentence with him. On the way to the underworld, Inana granted eternal life and death to both Dumuzi and Geshtinanna. For half of each year Inana and Dumuzi were together, while Geshtinanna took Dumuzi's place. When Dumuzi joined Inana, the milk flowed, the crops ripened and the fruit trees blossomed. During the barren months, however, Dumuzi had to return to the realm of Ereshkigal.

In ancient Sumer, a ceremony took place each year in which the king of each city would impersonate Dumuzi and the chief priestess would assume the role of Inana. The couple would take part in a marriage ritual, which was believed to ensure fertility and prosperity.

INARAS features in Hittite mythology as the goddess who helped bring about the death of the monstrous dragon or serpent *ILLUYANKAS*. She is sometimes said to be the daughter of the weather god *TARU*. When Taru failed to overcome Illuyankas, Inaras devised a plot to bring about the monster's downfall. She prepared a marvellous feast, then asked a mortal, *HUPASIYAS*, to help her in her task. Hupasiyas agreed, on condition that she sleep with him.

Once she had carried out his request, Inaras invited the dragon, together with his offspring, to attend the banquet. When the monsters had eaten and drunk their fill, they found they were unable to squeeze back into their underground home. Hupasiyas then bound Illuyankas with a rope, and Taru killed him. Inaras built Hupasiyas a house in gratitude for his help. Then she said, "Farewell! I am now going out. Do not look out of the window; for if you look out, you will see your wife and children." When 20 days had passed, Hupasiyas threw open the window and saw his family. As soon as Inaras returned from her journey, Hupasiyas begged her to let him go home, whereupon the goddess killed him.

ISHTAR, the goddess of love and fertility, was a fearsome, often violent, deity, sometimes known as the "Lady of Battles". The Babylonian form of the Sumerian goddess *INANA*, she was the guardian spirit of life and the creator of wisdom. Her symbol was the eight-pointed star. Although she had countless lovers, she usually treated them cruelly.

On one momentous occasion, Ishtar descended to the underworld realm of her sister *ERESHKIGAL*. However, Ereshkigal

INANA (left), often identified with Ishtar, the goddess of love and war, is shown here with Anubanini, king of the Lullubians.

ISHTAR (right), the Babylonian goddess of love and war, had countless lovers, both men and gods, but was fickle and cruel. (ILLUSTRATION FROM LEWIS SPENCE'S MYTHS OF BABYLONIA AND ASSYRIA.)

cursed her sister, who subsequently died. As a result of Ishtar's death, the earth became infertile and neither birds nor beasts nor human beings mated. *EA*, the water god, eventually managed to save Ishtar by using his magic incantations, but Ereshkigal demanded she be given someone in her sister's stead. It was finally decided that *TAMMUZ*, her husband, should replace her for six months of each year.

Uruk or Erech, Ishtar's holy city, was called the town of the sacred courtesans, for prostitution formed part of her cult and she protected harlots, as well as alehouses. The personification of the planet Venus, Ishtar was sometimes believed to be the daughter of the moon god, *SIN*, sometimes of the sky god *ANU*. (See also *DYING AND RISING GODS; SACRED ANIMALS*)

ISHTAR (left) became the principal goddess of the Babylonians and Assyrians. Like Inana, she was identified with Venus, the evening star. (ALABASTER, 2800–2300 BC, SYRIA.)

ISHTAR (right), in her violent form as "Lady of Battles", is shown heavily armed and mounted on a lion.

ISIS, the Egyptian mother goddess, was the daughter of *GEB* and *NUT*, and the sister and consort of *OSIRIS*. She is usually depicted with huge, sheltering wings, and she is sometimes regarded as a personification of the throne. The hieroglyph for her name is the image of a throne, and her lap came to be seen as the throne of Egypt.

Isis helped Osiris to civilize Egypt by teaching women to grind corn as well as how to spin and weave. She also taught people how to cure illness and instituted the rite of marriage. When Osiris left Egypt on his world travels, Isis ruled the country wisely and well in his stead. Aspects of the myth of Isis occur in various Egyptian texts, and were assembled into a single narrative by Plutarch in the first century AD.

On hearing of Osiris's death at the hands of the evil god *SETH*, Isis was distraught. She cut off her hair, put on mourning clothes and set off in search of his body. A group of children told Isis they had seen the chest that enclosed Osiris's body floating down the Nile and out into the sea. It was eventually washed up underneath a beautiful tree on the shores of Byblos in the Lebanon. The tree immediately began to grow, so quickly that it had soon enclosed the coffin in its trunk. Hearing of the astonishing tree, the king of Byblos ordered it to be cut down and brought to his palace, where it was used to support the roof.

News of the remarkable tree rapidly spread. Isis immediately guessed what had happened and rushed to Byblos where, after disguising herself, she sat by a well in the city centre. When some of the queen's servants came to fetch water from the well, Isis braided their hair for them, breathing on it such beautiful perfume that a short

ISIS (above) is usually depicted as a woman seated on a throne. She wears a headdress and huge wings which are outspread, protecting Egypt and its people. (SARCOPHAGUS OF RAMESES III, GRANITE.)

ISIS (left) was the sister and consort of Osiris, the murdered god. She sought his body throughout the land of Egypt when he was slain by the evil god Seth.

while later the queen sent for the stranger and made her the nurse of her child.

Each night, Isis placed the queen's child in the fire of immortality while she transformed herself into a swallow and flew around the pillar that enclosed Osiris's corpse. One evening, the queen came into the room and saw her son lying in the flames. She was so horrified that she let out a piercing scream, thereby causing her child to lose his chance of immortality. Isis then revealed her true identity and asked to be given the pillar.

Her wish was granted, and so at last she recovered Osiris's corpse. The goddess carried the body of Osiris back to Egypt where she hid it in a swamp. However, Seth discovered the body and cut it into 14 pieces, which he then scattered up and down the country. With the help of several other gods, Isis located all the pieces, except for the penis, which had been swallowed by a fish. According to one version of the story, Isis then reassembled the body and, using her healing and magical powers, restored Osiris to life. Before departing to the underworld, Osiris and Isis conceived a child, *HORUS*.

Isis became so famous throughout Egypt, and beyond, that in time she absorbed the qualities of almost all the other goddesses. She was a great mother goddess, a bird goddess, a goddess of the underworld who brought life to the dead and a goddess of the primeval waters. Her following spread beyond Egypt to Greece and throughout the Roman Empire. She was worshipped for more than 3,000 years, from before 3000 BC until well into Christian times. Her cult, and many of her images, passed directly on to the figure of the Virgin Mary.

ISKUR was a Hittite weather god who controlled the rain and thunderstorms. The "King of Heaven", he assisted the earthly king in battles and was represented sitting on two mountain gods or riding on a chariot drawn by bulls, his sacred animals. His attributes were a club and shafts of lightning, and his sacred number was ten.

JAHWEH see *YAHWEH*.

JAM see *YIMA*.

JAMM see *YAM*.

JEHOVAH see *YAHWEH*.

JEMSHID see *YIMA*.

JIBRIL see *GABRIEL*.

THE KA'ABA, or "Square House" is an oblong stone building, draped with black silk, which contains the sacred Black Stone of Islam. Situated within the mosque at Mecca, Islam's holiest city, the Ka'aba symbolizes the meeting of heaven and earth, and was an important shrine long before the time of the Prophet Muhammad (c. AD 570–632). It contained many images of gods and goddesses from the Arabian pantheon.

According to the Qur'an, the Ka'aba was rebuilt by *ABRAHAM* for the worship of the one true god – *ALLAH* – but the Meccans had enshrined a number of idols, the "Daughters of Allah", within it. Muhammad cleansed the Ka'aba of its idols and ordered that all prayers be directed to the structure. In pre-Islamic times, a four-month truce was called each year between the warring tribes of Arabia, and people from different tribes and towns would visit the shrine and circle round the structure.

Today, it is the sacred duty of all Muslim followers to try to make at least one pilgrimage to Mecca, specifically to the Ka'aba, in their lives. This pilgrimage is known as the hajj, and is one of the "Five Pillars of Islam". Its rites include seven circumambulations of the Ka'aba and, if possible, kissing the Black Stone.

Within Islam, the Black Stone is traditionally the place where Hagar conceived Ishmael, the ancestor of the Arabian people. Apocryphal stories abound as to its origins. One tale tells how it was once the most trustworthy of God's angels. God therefore placed the angel in the Garden of Eden, so that it might remind *ADAM* of his promise to God. However, with the Fall, Adam forgot his promise, and God

THE KA'ABA or "Square House" is an oblong stone building draped with black silk which contains the sacred Black Stone of Islam. (HAJJ CERTIFICATE, 1432.)

turned the angel into a white pearl. The pearl rolled towards Adam and then miraculously turned back into the angel once more. The angel reminded Adam of his promise, whereupon Adam kissed it. God then turned the angel into the Black Stone, to symbolize a world into which evil has entered. Adam carried the Black Stone across the world until he reached Mecca. There, the angel Gabriel told Adam to build the Ka'aba and to place the Black Stone within the structure.

Another story tells how the Abyssinian general Abraha determined to destroy the Ka'aba but was unable to enter the city of Mecca because the elephant upon which he was riding refused to move. Eventually, the general's army was forced to retreat.

KAMRUSEPAS see *TELEPINU*.

KERESASPA, according to some traditions within Iranian mythology, was the hero who would finally kill the monstrous dragon *AZHI DAHAKA*. Keresaspa was renowned for numerous brave deeds, and it is also told how he once went into battle against the vast bird Kamak, whose huge wings had covered the sky and thus prevented the fertilizing rain from reaching earth. Another monster to die at the hands of Keresaspa was Gandarewa, a demon who lived in the water and constantly threatened to swallow all that was good in creation.

KERET, the king of Sidon, was said to be a son of *EL*, the supreme god of the Ugaritic pantheon. A legend describing Keret's exploits was contained in texts dating from the 14th century BC, which were discovered in 1929 at Ras Shamra in Syria, on the site of the ancient city of Ugarit.

Keret had been married to seven wives, but all of them had died, and the king was despairing of ever fathering an heir to the throne. At this point, El appeared and ordered Keret to lead his army into battle against Sidon's enemies. Keret was terrified. He locked himself away and burst into tears. However, in a dream he discovered that he was to father a son, and this encouraged him to undertake the campaign. Afterwards, Keret took a wife and promised that he would give the goddess Asherat (see *ASTARTE*) presents of silver and gold in thanks. El blessed the king and said that he would father eight sons.

The children were born in due course, but Keret failed to keep his vow to Asherat. He became seriously ill and vegetation withered throughout his kingdom. A ceremony was held in the palace of the rain and fertility god, *BAAL*. The rains appeared, and Keret recovered from his illness.

KHNUM, an Egyptian creator god, was said to have fashioned the world on his potter's wheel. His name means "Moulder". The god is frequently depicted as a ram-headed man sitting in front of a potter's wheel on which stands the being he has created. Khnum made the gods as well as people. He was also said to control the annual inundation of the river Nile.

In one story, the historical sage IMHOTEP, a minister and architect to King Zoser in the third millennium BC, was consulted by the ruler about the cause of a seven-year famine. The Nile was failing to rise high enough to irrigate the fields, and the people were starving. Imhotep told Zoser that he should make offerings to Khnum. The king did as he was advised, whereupon Khnum appeared to him in a dream and promised him that he would release the waters. That year, the kingdom enjoyed a splendid harvest. (See also SACRED ANIMALS)

KINGU was a demon of ancient Mesopotamia. He was either the son or husband of TIAMAT, the mother goddess and monster of chaos. Kingu sided with his mother in her tremendous battle against MARDUK, leading an army of ferocious monsters into battle. However, like Tiamat, Kingu was

eventually slain by Marduk. According to one traditional story, Marduk mixed Kingu's blood with earth and used the clay to mould the first human beings. Kingu then went to live in the underworld kingdom of ERESHKIGAL, along with the other deities who had sided with Tiamat.

KHNUM (far left), the creator god, was portrayed with a ram's head as a symbol of potency and virility.

KHNUM (left) was said to have made men and women on his potter's wheel, and was also responsible for the flooding of the Nile.

KISHAR see ANSHAR.

THE KORYBANTES, or Corybantes, were the companions of CYBELE, the great mother of Phrygian mythology. They performed frenzied dances, took part in orgiastic revelries and were believed to have the power both to induce and to heal madness.

According to one tradition, they were the offspring of the Greek god Zeus, who impregnated the earth by falling on it as rain. According to another story, they were the offspring of the Greek deities Thalia and Apollo.

L

KUBABA (left), at first a local goddess of Carchemish, later became the neo-Hittite mother goddess. (BASALT RELIEF, CARCHEMISH, SYRIA, 9TH CENTURY BC.)

KOTAR see KOTHAR.

KOTHAR, or Kotar, was the divine craftsman or blacksmith of Phoenician mythology. Lord of magic spells and incantations, he appears in myths dating from the 14th century BC discovered at Ras Shamra in Syria, the site of the ancient city of Ugarit. Kothar created a marvellous bow for the hero AHAT. It was made from twisted horns and shaped like a serpent. The servant of the supreme god EL, Kothar helped to build a palace for BAAL, the god of rain and fertility.

KUBABA was an ancient goddess of Carchemish in Asia Minor. As a local goddess, she had only a minor role to play in the mythology of the region. In due course, however, she became the chief goddess of the neo-Hittite kingdoms and took on the characteristics of a mother goddess, whose attributes included a

KUBABA holds a mirror, one of the attributes inherited from her by the Phrygian goddess Cybele. (BASALT RELIEF, CARCHEMISH, SYRIA, 9TH CENTURY BC.)

mirror and a pomegranate. Her name, as well as some of her attributes, were taken over by the Phrygians for their mother goddess CYBELE, whose attributes also included a mirror and pomegranate. In Upper Mesopotamia she was known as Gubaba.

KUMARBI was the father of the gods in the mythology of the Hurrians, a people who lived in the mountainous regions south of the Caspian Sea and whose beliefs had a huge influence on those of the Hittites. Before acceding to the throne, Kumarbi had to depose ANU, to whom he had bowed down and ministered for nine years. At the end of the nine-year period, Kumarbi attacked Anu, who immediately flew up into the sky like a bird soaring to heaven. However, Kumarbi pulled Anu down by his feet and and bit off his penis. Anu told Kumarbi not to rejoice, for he had been impregnated by his sperm and would bear three terrible gods. These deities are believed to have been different aspects of the weather god TESHUB.

Kumarbi was eventually deposed by his son, Teshub. Kumarbi determined on revenge and, after seeking the help of the sea, proceeded to father another son. Known as ULLIKUMMI, he was made of diorite stone and was placed on the shoulders of the giant Upelluri, who lived in the middle of the sea. Teshub attacked Ullikummi, but he was unsuccessful in his onslaught and was forced to abdicate. Although the end of the myth is missing, it is widely agreed that Teshub eventually succeeded in defeating Kumarbi and regaining the throne.

KURUNTA was a Hittite god, generally believed to have been associated with the countryside. He appeared in a version of the myth of the disappearing god, HAHHIMAS, which describes the decline and death of all living

things. The weather god TARU sought to prevent Kurunta from being beguiled by Hahhimas, who paralysed people into inaction, but even Kurunta, a "child of the open country", fell prey to him. Kurunta was depicted standing on a stag, his sacred animal, and holding a hare and a falcon. Models of stags have been found in tombs dating from the third millennium BC.

LELWANI was originally a Hittite god of the underworld, referred to as "King". Over time, he seems to have developed into a female deity. She lived in the dark earth, and her shrines were connected with charnel houses and mausoleums.

LEVIATHAN was a ferocious monster of Phoenician mythology. His name means "Coiled". The figure of Leviathan drew on the Canaanite Lotan, a seven-headed monster killed by ANAT, as well as on the chaos monster TIAMAT of Mesopotamian mythology.

LEVIATHAN, the fearsome sea monster, was an expression of the chaos from which Yahweh protected humankind. (ILLUSTRATION BY GUSTAVE DORÉ FROM PARADISE LOST, 1866.)

In the Old Testament, Leviathan is the chaos dragon who is overcome by YAHWEH. He is referred to in Isaiah as the "crooked serpent", and in the Book of Job, God says, "His heart is as firm as a stone; yea as hard as a piece of the nether millstone." The lashings of his tail "maketh the deep to boil like a pot . . . Upon earth there is not his like, who is made without fear. He beholdeth all high things: he is a king over all the children of pride."

In apocalyptic writings, as well as in Christianity, the devil is said to manifest himself as the serpent Leviathan. In the apocryphal Book of Enoch, he appears as a vast creature, which inhabits "the abyss over the fountains of the waters." Leviathan's jaws were sometimes regarded as the very gates of hell. (See also SERPENTS AND DRAGONS)

GATEWAYS TO THE GODS

THE EGYPTIANS BELIEVED THAT, on the death of the pharaoh, the sun god Ra would strengthen the rays of the sun to enable the king to ascend, as if he were climbing a heavenly staircase. The pyramid shape symbolized such a ramp, and the earliest pyramids were indeed designed in steps. Seen as a stylized mound, or hill, the pyramid also echoed the primeval hill which had risen out of the waters of Nun at the beginning of creation. The Mesopotamian equivalent of the pyramid was the ziggurat, a stepped structure that also rose skywards on a huge scale, with ramps and stairways connecting the levels and leading up to an altar at the top. The ancient builders of these colossal monuments saw the sun as an all-powerful creator and their ruler as a personification of the god. Their buildings, soaring skywards, connected them with the deity while glorifying his mortal embodiment on earth.

THE ZIGGURAT (above) of Ur was a temple dedicated to the Sumerian moon god Nanna, who measured time and brought fertility to the land. Built from rough, unbaked brick, it originally shone with a facing of glazed tiles. Long flights of steps connected the different levels and ultimately led to an altar at the very top: the ziggurat's function was to raise the worshippers closer to the sky deities.

ZIGGURATS (left) were built in most major Mesopotamian cities. They were huge, stepped pyramids, surmounted by a temple where offerings were made, to which it was thought that the deity would descend to communicate with his or her devotees. The temple of Marduk in Babylon, seven storeys high, was possibly the inspiration for the biblical story of the Tower of Babel. (OTTO GIRARD, A ZIGGURAT RECONSTRUCTED, 19TH CENTURY.)

ANUBIS (above) presided over mummification and funeral rites. Since the Egyptians regarded the afterlife as a continuation of their earthly existence, the correct preservation of the corpse was vital. Detailed incantations, designed as a guide to the underworld, accompanied the body, at first carved inside tombs, and later written on an illustrated papyrus scroll known as the Book of the Dead. (THE BOOK OF THE DEAD OF KHENSUMOSE, 11TH–10TH CENTURY BC.)

THE PYRAMIDS' (below) vast size attested to the Egyptians' overriding concern with the continuation of life after death. Tens of thousands of men laboured for decades to construct them, under the direction of a single architect, who was given the title of "Overseer of All the King's Works". Most of the stone was quarried locally, and the huge blocks were hauled on sleds up ramps that rose higher and more steeply as the pyramid grew.

THE TOWER OF BABEL (above) was said to have been built on the plain of Shinar in Babylonia, according to the Bible, by the descendants of Noah, with the intention of reaching up to heaven. Yahweh, the god of the Israelites, disapproved of this product of human pride. He thwarted their plan by confusing their speech so that they no longer understood one another's instructions. The tower, and the planned city, were abandoned, and the people scattered. (MEDIEVAL MANUSCRIPT REPRODUCED IN STRUTT'S ANTIQUITIES, 1773.)

THE PYRAMIDS (above) of Giza were regarded by the Greeks as one of the Seven Wonders of the World, and are the only one of the seven to have survived virtually intact. Their awesome size and mysterious nature made it difficult to believe that they were the work of human hands. Imhotep, the architect of the first pyramid – and the first stone building in Egypt – achieved great renown by his feat: by the Late Period, 2,000 years after his death, he had become a god. (ENGRAVING BY JACQUES PICART FROM THE SEVEN WONDERS OF THE WORLD, 17TH CENTURY.)

M

LILITH is flanked by owls, her sacred animals. Created with Adam, she rejected his authority and consorted with demons. She wears a crown of lunar horns and a rainbow necklace. (TERRACOTTA.)

from earth. However, instead of using clean earth, Yahweh made her from filth and sediments.

Lilith originated in Sumerian mythology as a goddess of desolation. She is also associated with the Babylonian demon Lilitu, who preyed upon men. (See also *SERPENTS AND DRAGONS*)

LILITU see *LILITH*.

LUCIFER see *SATAN*.

MAAT was the Egyptian goddess of truth, justice and harmony. A daughter of the sun god, *RA*, she ruled over the judgment of the dead in the throne room of *OSIRIS*. Each person, when they died, had to appear before the 42 judges of the dead and declare whether they were innocent or guilty of numerous crimes. The soul of the dead person would be weighed on a pair of scales against the goddess, represented by a single ostrich feather. The scales were held by the jackal-headed god, *ANUBIS*, and their verdict was recorded by Maat's consort, the moon god, *THOTH*. If the heart was weighed down by crimes, the terrifying female monster Ammut, part crocodile, part hippopotamus, part lion, would devour the dead person. If, however, the deceased had lived "with Maat in his heart", and was thus pure and virtuous, he became a spirit, and could live with the gods to fight against the serpent *APEP*.

Maat was depicted wearing on her head the feather that was said to be put in the scales of judgment. As the "Breath of Life", she was often pictured ministering to the *PHARAOHS* by holding the ankh, a symbol of life, to their noses. All human beings were intended to live "by Maat, in Maat and for Maat."

LILITH, according to Hebrew legend, was the first woman to be created. She was portrayed as part snake, part woman and wearing wings. *YAHWEH* blamed her for having tempted *EVE* to reveal the mysteries of the Garden of Eden to *ADAM*. In the Old Testament, she is the demon who disturbs the night. Her name means "Storm Goddess", or "She of the Night". The owl was her sacred creature.

According to Talmudic legend, Lilith was created at the same time as Adam. She refused to lie down beneath him, believing herself to be his equal, and flew away to the desert. There, she consorted with demons and became the mother of numerous other demons, at the rate of more than a hundred each day. God sent three angels to bring Lilith back from the desert, but she refused. The angels threatened to drown her, but she warned them that she had the power to kill children. Eventually she agreed not to harm children: "Whenever I shall see you or your names or your images on an amulet . . ." Lilith then wandered the world, looking for unprotected children who deserved to be punished because of the sins of their fathers. She killed them by smiling at them.

According to another tradition, Lilith desired to join the ranks of the cherubim, but God forced her to descend to the earth. When Lilith saw that Adam already had a partner, Eve, she attempted to return to the cherubim but instead found herself cast out into the desert. One Hebrew myth tells how Yahweh made Lilith, like Adam,

MAAT, goddess of truth and justice, is depicted wearing a single ostrich feather, which is an ideogram of her name. (TOMB OF HUREMHEB, EGYPT.)

THE MALA'IKA, according to Islamic belief, are angels. They are sometimes said to be made from light and are believed to be superior to ordinary humankind but inferior to the prophets. The four chief angels are Jibril or *GABRIEL*, the holy spirit; Mikha'il, the guardian of the Jews; Israfil, the angel who will sound the trumpet at the resurrection; and Arazil, the "Angel of Death". *IBLIS* is either regarded as the fallen arazil or as one of the *DJINN*.

MANAT, or Menat, was a goddess of pre-Islamic Arabia who was worshipped in the region between the holy cities Mecca and Medina. She was believed to be one of the three daughters of *ALLAH*, the supreme god, the others being *AL-UZZA* and *AL-LAT*. As a goddess of fate, Manat had control over human destiny.

MANDAH was the name given to a pre-Islamic group of Arabian gods who were concerned with irrigation as well as being protective deities.

MARDUK, the chief god of Babylon, was the oldest son of *EA*, the water god. Born in the waters of *APSU*, the primordial, fresh-water ocean, Marduk was originally regarded as a fertility or agricultural deity whose attribute was an agricultural implement with a triangular blade, called a "mar". However, he gained a reputation as a fearless warrior and was usually depicted armed for battle. His name means "Calf of the Sun God", and he was associated with the planet Jupiter. This most splendid of gods apparently had four eyes and four ears, and fire blazed forth when his lips moved.

In time, Marduk's reputation for bravery grew to such an extent that he was chosen by the gods to attack the terrifying monster *TIAMAT*. He was given a thunderbolt as a weapon and also equipped himself with his bow, spear and mace. After a ferocious battle, Marduk slaughtered Tiamat: "When Tiamat opened her mouth to consume him, he drove in the evil wind that she close not her lips. As the fierce winds charged her belly, Her body was distended and her mouth was wide open. He released the arrow, it tore her belly, It cut through her insides, splitting the heart. Having thus subdued her, he extinguished her life."

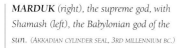

MARDUK (right), the supreme god, with Shamash (left), the Babylonian god of the sun. (AKKADIAN CYLINDER SEAL, 3RD MILLENNIUM BC.)

The great god cast down Tiamat's carcass, stood upon it and, after slicing her body in two, thrust one half upwards to form the vault of the heavens and pushed the other half down to form the floor of the deep. Thus, the earth and sky were created. Marduk then divided the year up into 12 months, made the constellations and appointed the sun and moon to their places in the sky. He then addressed his father saying "Blood I will mass and cause bones to be. I will establish a savage, 'man' shall be his name."

The gods tied up *KINGU*, who had sided with his mother, Tiamat, in the battle, and severed his blood vessels. Out of his blood, which they mixed with clay, they fashioned human beings.

Before agreeing to attack Tiamat, Marduk had successfully persuaded the gods that, if he rose to the challenge, he should be granted additional powers, including the ability to determine fates and the right to pardon or kill captives taken in battle. After killing the monster, he was awarded 50 titles, each of which corresponded to a powerful divine attribute. In this manner, Marduk came to absorb all the other gods and to symbolize total divinity. He even threatened *ANU*'s status as supreme god, taking from him the power of his dignity.

According to one tale, the evil genies were annoyed by the moon god, *SIN*, whose light revealed their wrongdoings for all to see. The genies, together with *SHAMASH*, *ISHTAR* and *ADAD*, devised a plot whereby they eventually succeeded in eclipsing Sin's light. However, Marduk, displaying no fear whatsoever, simply overcame the conspirators and put them to flight. (See also *SACRED ANIMALS*; *SERPENTS AND DRAGONS*)

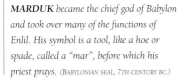

MARDUK became the chief god of Babylon and took over many of the functions of Enlil. His symbol is a tool, like a hoe or spade, called a "mar", before which his priest prays. (BABYLONIAN SEAL, 7TH CENTURY BC.)

MASHYA AND MASHYOI

were the first human couple of ancient Iranian mythology. In some traditions, they were said to have been born from the seed of *GAYOMART*, the primeval man, after it had lain in the soil for 40 years. Their first act was to walk, their second to eat. Then, however, they were sent a thought by a demon and, as a result, they became victims of *ANGRA MAINYU*, the principle of darkness. However, the good spirits continued to protect them. In time, Mashya and Mashyoi begat seven couples. One of these couples, Siyamek and Siyameki, became the parents of *HAOSHYANGHA* and of Fravak and Fravakain, who were said to be the ancestors of the 15 different peoples into which humankind was divided.

MEHUERET see *NEITH*.

MEN, a Phrygian moon god, was

said to rule over both the underworld and the heavens. He was attributed with the good health of plants and animals and was referred to as Tyrannos or "Master".

MENAT see *MANAT*.

MIN, an ancient and popular

Egyptian god, was always depicted with an erect phallus and with a flail raised in his right hand. On his

MIN (left), the god of roads and travellers, wore upon his head a crown decorated with two upright plumes. (RELIEF, KARNAK.)

head he wore a crown decorated with two tall, straight plumes. It is thought that Min may originally have been worshipped as a creator deity, but in classical times he was venerated as the god of roads and protector of those who travelled through the desert. His main cult centre was at Koptos, a centre for commercial travellers, and prayers were offered to the god before the travellers embarked on their expeditions. Min was also a god of fertility and growth, and a protector of crops. His main feast was known as the Feast of the Steps. Seated on his step, the god received the first sheaf of the harvest, which had been cut by the king.

MINUCHER, according to

ancient Iranian mythology, was a descendant of *FERIDUN*, the great hero. When Feridun grew old he gave each of his three sons, Selm, Tur and Irej, a share of his kingdom. However, Selm and Tur plotted to take Irej's share from him. Irej was willing simply to give his brothers his part of the kingdom, and so he came before them unarmed. Without hearing what he had to say, Tur struck him over the head with a golden chair and then slashed him with his sword from head to foot until Irej's body

was streaming with blood. Tur tore Irej's head from his body, filled his skull with musk and amber, and sent it to Feridun. The king, who was waiting for his youngest son to return home, was stricken with grief when he heard what had happened and sought revenge.

Eventually Irej's grandson *MINUCHER* attacked and killed Selm and Tur in a bloody and ferocious battle. Feridun then died, leaving the throne to Minucher.

MITHRA, known in Indian

mythology as Mitra, was originally a god of contracts and friendship. In Iran he developed into the protector of truth. Before the time of *ZOROASTER*, the religious reformer, Mithra was often

associated with *AHURA MAZDA*, the principle of good. Mithra was the light: he was believed to ride his golden chariot, the sun, across the sky, drawn by four white horses. He had 10,000 ears and eyes, possessed both strength and knowledge, and was renowned for his bravery in battle. The god was able to bless those who worshipped him with victory over their enemies as well as wisdom, but he showed no mercy to his foes. As a god of fertility, he caused the rain to fall and the plants to grow.

According to one tradition, Mithra, as the sun, formed a link between Ahura Mazda and *ANGRA MAINYU*, the principle of darkness. This supposition was built on the understanding that the sun marked the continual revolutions of light and dark. Under Zoroaster's reforms to Iranian religion, Mithra was ousted from power, and Ahura

MITHRA was a forerunner of the Graeco-Roman god Mithras, shown here. Mithra was worshipped in underground shrines, many of them decorated with a relief showing him slaying the bull Geush Urvan. (MITHRAEUM OF SIDON, 4TH CENTURY AD.)

MOSES (left) was given the Ten Commandments on Mount Sinai. Here he presents them to the Hebrew people. (ILLUSTRATION BY H. PISAN.)

MOSES (right) loosens his sandal on Mount Horeb, or Sinai, obeying God's command from the burning bush. (MOSAIC, SAN VITALE, RAVENNA, ITALY.)

Mazda was given the position of supreme deity. Although, in the fourth century BC, Mithra returned as the focus of an extremely popular cult, Zoroastrians continued to give him no credence.

At his birth, Mithra was said to have emerged from a rock armed with a knife and a torch. He was worshipped in underground shrines, almost all of which were decorated with a relief showing him slaying the bull GEUSH URVAN, from whose corpse all plants and animals arose.

Regular sacrifices, particularly of bulls, were made to Mithra, in the belief that the fertility of nature would thereby be ensured. In the first century BC, when the Roman Empire expanded into western Asia, Mithra was assimilated into Graeco-Roman belief as the god Mithras.

MOLECH see MOLOCH.

MOLOCH, or Molech, was the name of an Ammonite god to whom human sacrifices were made. The Ammonites occupied the southern part of modern Jordan and were descended from Lot, who appears in the Old Testament as the nephew of the patriarch ABRAHAM. In the Second Book of Kings, Moloch is described as the "abomination of the children of Ammon."

Many Israelites are believed to have consecrated their children to Moloch by throwing them into the flames. It is sometimes argued that, rather than being the name of a god, Moloch refers simply to the sacrificial ritual. The children were burnt in a place called Tophet, in

the valley of Hinnom, which had been built for the explicit purpose of sacrificial rituals.

The king was sometimes regarded as the son of Moloch, and the phrase "to the molech" may have meant "for the sake or life of the king" and referred to the sacrifice of a child conceived at a sacred marriage rite. Other research suggests that Moloch may have been the god Baal-Hammon who was worshipped at Tyre and Carthage.

MOSES was a great Hebrew prophet who is generally believed to have lived in the 13th century BC and who fulfilled many of the traditional functions of the mythic

hero. He was the agent of God in delivering the tribes of Israel from their bondage in Egypt, and he presented them with the law establishing God's covenant with them. He is traditionally regarded as having written a portion of the Pentateuch, the first five books of the Bible.

During the period of the Israelites' exile in Egypt, Moses survived a decree to kill all male children by being hidden in the bulrushes. He was discovered there by an Egyptian princess and was brought up in the royal palace. Later, during a period in exile, Moses was grazing his flock when an angel of God appeared to him in

a flame of fire, which issued from a bush. Speaking from the centre of the fire, the voice of God told Moses that he was called "I am that I am", which the Hebrews expressed by the four letters YHWH or JHWH, later pronounced as "YAHWEH".

In a later episode, recounted in the Book of Exodus, Moses led his people out of Egypt, and God drew back the Red Sea for them, so that they could walk across to freedom. On Mount Sinai, Moses received the Ten Commandments, written on tablets of stone, and the people of Israel made a pact, or covenant, with their new deity, Yahweh.

N

MOT, according to Phoenician mythology, was the god of death, drought and infertility. He ruled over the underworld and over the countryside when the ground lay dry. On one important occasion, *BAAL*, the god of rain, thunderstorms and fertility, challenged Mot to a contest, and banished death to the barren wastelands. In response, Mot challenged Baal to come to his underground home and eat mud, the food of the dead. Baal accepted the challenge but died as a result. The goddess *ANAT*, furious with grief, visited Mot to seek the release of her brother and consort. She carried off Baal's corpse and, when Mot refused to restore him to life, she killed Mot in a ritual slaughter: "With her sickle she cleaves him. With her flail she beats him. With fire she grills him. With her mill she

grinds him. In the fields she scatters him, to consume his leaven, so that he no longer withholds his share [of the crop]." The supreme god *EL* learned in a dream that Baal was to come back to life: he saw the skies dripping with oil and streams running with honey.

The story of Mot and Baal provides a dramatic account of the agricultural cycle, its periods of dryness and death under the rule of Mot, alternating with the revival of the land's fertility when Baal was brought back to life. According to the Jewish historian Philo (*c*. 30 BC–AD 45), Mot was created at the beginning of time when the dark forces of chaos mingled with air. However, Mot was usually regarded as the son of *EL*.

NAMTAR see *RESHEF*.

NEITH, the Egyptian great mother, was envisaged as the great weaver who wove the world with her shuttle. (TOMB OF RAMESES I.)

NANNA see *SIN*.

NASR, an Arabian deity of pre-Islamic times, is mentioned in the Qur'an. He was one of the five idols who were erected by the descendants of Cain, the others being *WADD*, Sowa, Yaghut and Ya'uk. His name is translated as either "Vulture" or "Eagle".

NEBTHET see *NEPHTHYS*.

NEITH, the great mother of the Egyptians, was originally the local goddess of Sais, situated in the Nile delta of Lower Egypt. She was also a warrior goddess and a goddess of the home. As a goddess of war, who was believed to march into battle ahead of the soldiers, her symbol was a shield with crossed arrows. She was often said to be the mother of *SEBEK*, the crocodile god, and was also said to have created the terrible cosmic serpent *APEP* by spitting into *NUN*, the watery abyss.

Neith came to be regarded as the mother of all the gods, and in particular of *RA*, and was sometimes seen as the celestial cow, Mehueret, who gave birth to the sky before life began. Neith also became the protectress of the dead. She is sometimes depicted offering them food and drink on their arrival in the underworld.

NEKHBET, the vulture goddess of Upper Egypt, protected the ruling pharaoh and suckled him and the royal children. (TEMPLE OF HATSHEPSUT, EGYPT.)

NEKHBET was the vulture goddess of Upper Egypt. She was often depicted with her wings outspread, holding the symbols of eternity in her claws. Nekhbet was widely regarded as a mother goddess who looked after the ruling *PHARAOH*, along with *WADJET*, the cobra goddess of Lower Egypt.

NEPHTHYS, or Nebthet, the consort of the evil Egyptian god *SETH*, was a daughter of the earth god *GEB* and sky goddess, *NUT*. Her name means "Mistress of the House or Castle". The goddess was sometimes regarded as a symbol of the desert edge; often barren but occasionally, after a flood, fruitful.

Nephthys and Seth had no children of their own. However, according to one tradition Nephthys plied her brother *OSIRIS* with drink, seduced him and conceived a child. In some stories, the baby she gave birth to was *ANUBIS*, the jackal-headed god. When Seth murdered Osiris, Nephthys immediately abandoned her husband and helped her sister *ISIS* to embalm Osiris's corpse. The two goddesses then took the form of kites and hovered over the body, protecting it while it awaited burial. Nephthys thus came to be associated with the dead.

NEPHTHYS with her sister Isis. After the death of Osiris, Nephthys helped Isis prepare him for burial. The sisters are often portrayed protecting the bodies of the dead. (PAPYRUS, EGYPT. C. 1300 BC.)

NERGAL see *ERESHKIGAL.*

NINGAL see *SIN.*

NINGIRSU see *NINURTA.*

NINHURSAGA, the Sumerian goddess known as "Lady of the Great Mountain" or "Lady of the Stony Ground", was sometimes referred to as the mother of the gods, the great creative principle. As *NINLIL*, she was the wife of *ENLIL*, lord of the wind; and as Ninki, she was the wife of Enki (or *EA*), the god of water. Ninhursaga was said to nourish earthly kings with her milk, thereby making them divine. Many Mesopotamian rulers, including Nebuchadnezzar, called themselves her children.

The goddess was associated with birth; she was the power that gave shape to life in the womb and was the divine midwife of gods and mortals. However, she was also the stony ground that lies at the edges of the Arabian desert.

Enki and Ninki were believed to live together on the island of Dilmun, a paradise land sometimes thought to be present-day Bahrein. The divine couple had several children, and indeed, all the vegetation in the land was said to originate from their union. However, in time, Enki began to take a sexual interest in his daughters, whereupon Ninki fell into a terrifying rage. Retrieving Enki's semen from the body of Uttu, the spider goddess, she planted it in the ground. The seeds grew into eight plants. When Enki ate the plants, he was attacked by illness in eight parts of his body. Nobody but Ninki was able to cure him, which at length she did by placing him in her womb, from which he was reborn.

53

NINKI see *NINHURSAGA.*

NINLIL, the Sumerian grain goddess, was sometimes associated with the goddess *NINHURSAGA.* One day *ENLIL*, the god of the air, found Ninlil bathing in a canal near the city of Nippur and, unable to resist her beauty, raped her. In punishment, the gods banished Enlil from Nippur and sentenced him to death. Enlil departed for the land of the dead, but Ninlil followed him so that he should see her give birth to the son they had conceived. The child, when born, became the moon god, Nanna, or *SIN*. Enlil was overwhelmed with grief that his son would have to live with him in the land of the dead and tried to persuade Ninlil to have another child by him, who would act as Nanna's replacement while Nanna returned to the land of the living. Ninlil eventually agreed and in due course gave birth to three more children, thereby appeasing the underworld goddess *ERESHKIGAL* for the loss of Nanna.

NINURTA, or Ningirsu, was a Mesopotamian god of war. He was also associated with the irrigation of the land. Ninurta's warlike temperament prompted a vast army to rise up against him. All of nature joined in the battle, including the rocks and stones. Ninurta soon conquered his enemies. He rewarded those stones that had taken his side by giving them the power to shine and glitter, while those that had sided against him he left to be trodden underfoot.

In another story, Ninurta retrieved the tablets of destiny from the tempest bird, *ZU*. In some accounts, Ninurta is the son of *ENLIL* and *NINHURSAGA* and the husband of Gula, the goddess of healing. In early Sumerian tales, Ninurta took the form of Imdugud, the storm bird, but he gradually came to have human form. However, he was usually represented with wings, and when on the battlefield would still appear as a lion-headed storm bird.

NOAH is the hero of the Old Testament story of the flood. According to the Book of Genesis, God saw that humankind had become wicked and declared, "I will destroy man whom I have created from the face of the earth;

NINURTA, the Mesopotamian god of war, taking part in a New Year or creation ritual with the winged goddess, Ishtar, the water god, Ea, and the sun god, Shamash.
(AKKADIAN CYLINDER SEAL, C. 2400–2200 BC).

NOAH cursed Ham's son Canaan because Ham had seen "the nakedness of his father", Noah. This may be a later attempt to explain Canaan's subjugation to the tribes of Israel. (19TH CENTURY ENGRAVING.)

both man, and beast, and the creeping things, and the fowls of the air; for it repenteth me that I have made them." However, because Noah was a good and faithful man, God decided to save him, together with his family.

God instructed Noah to make an ark and to take into it two of every living thing. When the day of the flood arrived, water gushed from the ground, and the rain began to fall. For 40 days and 40 nights the torrent continued until

the entire earth was submerged. After some time had passed, Noah sent out a dove to see if the flood had abated but it returned to the ark. Eventually, another dove returned with an olive leaf in its mouth. God promised never again to flood the earth and offered the rainbow as a sign of good faith: "This is the token of the covenant which I make between me and you and every living creature that is with you, for perpetual generations: I do set my bow in the cloud."

Flood myths are found throughout the ancient world, from Greece to India. The story of a flood destroying earth appears in the epic of *GILGAMESH* as well as in the myth of the Sumerian water god Enki (see *EA*) and the hero

NOAH was instructed by God to build an ark and take into it two of every living thing, to preserve them from the destruction of the flood. (FRENCH BOOK ILLUSTRATION, C. 1260.)

Atrahasis, or Ziusadra.(See also *MYTHS OF THE FLOOD*)

UNDERWORLDS

THE MYTHOLOGY OF EVERY CULTURE included the idea that life in some way continued after death. The spirit might inhabit another physical body and live on earth again, or lead a perpetual existence in a murky netherworld. The concept of judgment invariably accompanied death and determined the future of the soul. A tribunal of gods or angels awaited the deceased to weigh up their conduct. The religion of the Egyptians was dominated by their funerary cult, but far from being obsessed with death itself, they saw it simply as a brief interruption. They aspired to an afterlife that was a continuation of their existence on earth in every respect, preserving their social status, family connections and even their physical possessions. Only for those who had failed to please the gods during their mortal lives, or who had not prepared themselves for their journey through the underworld with the proper rituals and incantations, was death really a termination.

OSIRIS (right) was originally a deity of vegetation and agriculture, but the myth of his death became central to his cult and raised his status to that of a great god. The pharaoh, who was considered to be an incarnation of Ra the sun god while he was alive, became identified with Osiris on his death. Osiris was depicted wearing the crown of Egypt, and carrying the royal insignia of the crook and flail, but was tightly wrapped in mummy cloths. As lord of the underworld, he presided over the judgment of the dead on their arrival in his realm. (WALL PAINTING FROM THE GRAVE OF SENNUTEM, 14TH CENTURY BC.)

MASHU (right) was a magic mountain which formed the boundary of the Mesopotamian underworld, into which the sun set each night. When the hero Gilgamesh visited the underworld in search of the immortal Utnapishtim, he had to pass through the gates of Mashu, guarded by fearsome scorpion gods. After a journey in total darkness, he emerged into an enchanted garden of precious stones. (ILLUSTRATION FROM GILGAMESH BY ZABELLE C BOYAJIAN, 1924.)

THE WEIGHING OF THE SOUL (above) was a decisive moment in the Egyptian journey to the underworld. The deceased was brought by Anubis before a panel of judges and his heart, where thought and memory resided, was weighed on the scales. It had to balance exactly with the goddess of truth, Maat. If it failed, the spirit was destroyed: the terrible Ammut, with the head of a crocodile and the mane of a lion, crouched by the scales waiting to eat the condemned. The ibis-headed god Thoth declared the result. (FROM THE BOOK OF THE DEAD OF HUNEFER, 13TH CENTURY BC.)

MUMMIFICATION (left) was practised to preserve a corpse so that life could continue after death, and this was the domain of the mortuary god, Anubis. He took the form of a black dog or jackal – the very animal who might scavenge a body that was incorrectly buried. The heart was the only internal organ left in the body, and it was protected by a scarab beetle bearing a spell that would keep it from confessing any sins during interrogation before Anubis. (WALL PAINTING FROM THE GRAVE OF SENNUTEM, 14TH CENTURY BC.)

O

NUN, according to Egyptian mythology, was the personification of the watery abyss that existed at the beginning of time and which contained the potential for all life.

According to one Egyptian creation myth, these formless, chaotic waters contained four pairs: Nun and Naunet, Kuk and Kauket, Huh and Hauhet, AMON and Amaunet. These pairs, known as the Ogdoad, symbolized the primeval waters. Eventually the four pairs formed an egg in the waters of Nun, and out of the egg burst a fabulous bird, or, according to some versions of the story, air. This bird was a manifestation of the creator god. According to one tradition, the sun god Atum rose from Nun in the form of a hill, a primeval mound, and gave birth to SHU, the god of air, and Tefnut, the goddess of moisture. Nun was depicted as a man standing in water, his arms raised to support the boat of the sun god. (See also MYTHS OF THE FLOOD)

NUSKU see SIN.

NUT, the Egyptian goddess of the sky, was the twin sister of the earth god, GEB. When, against RA's wishes, she married her brother, Ra was so enraged that he commanded SHU to separate the couple. Shu pushed Nut upwards to form the sky and Geb down to form the earth. Ra was so angry with Nut that he decreed that she would be unable to bear children in any month of the year. However, the god THOTH took pity on her. He challenged the moon to a game of draughts, and, when he won, took as his prize enough of the moon's light to create five new days. On each of these days, Nut bore a child: OSIRIS, SETH, ISIS, NEPHTHYS and, according to some versions of the tale, HORUS.

Another myth tells how Nut helped Ra to distance himself from human beings when he became disillusioned with their ways.

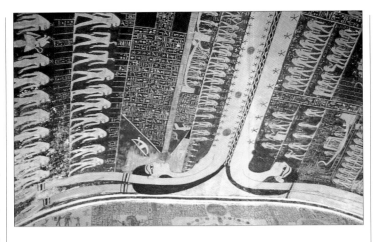

Taking the form of a cow, she raised the great god upwards on her back. However, the higher Nut rose, the dizzier she became, until she had to summon four gods to steady her legs. These gods became the pillars of the sky.

OG, according to Hebrew mythology, was one of the many giants who roamed the earth before the great flood that destroyed creation.

NUT, the Egyptian sky goddess, arches over the earth, formed by her consort, Geb. She balances on her outstretched fingers and toes, which touch the four cardinal points. (TOMB OF RAMESES VI.)

Of these giants, Og alone survived the flood. According to one story, the flood waters reached no higher than Og's ankles, and so he remained unharmed by the deluge. Other stories tell how NOAH allowed Og to sit on the roof of his ark while Noah fed him oxen.

After the flood had subsided, Og fell in love with Sarah, the wife of ABRAHAM, and jealously plotted against the patriarch. The enmity between Og and Abraham continued down the years, and it culminated in a battle with MOSES. After the great prophet had led the Israelites out of Egypt into the land of Canaan, he was forced to engage in numerous battles against the local people. One of these battles was against Edrei, a city ruled by Og. When the giant spotted the approaching forces, he lifted a mountain high above his head and was about to drop it on Moses and his followers when YAHWEH caused the monstrous missile to drop on to Og's own shoulders. The giant

NUT was depicted on funerary amulets which were attached to a mummy for protection. At death, the pharoah was said to pass into the body of Nut. A scarab was placed over the heart to keep it silent during the judgment of the dead.
(MUMMY ACCESSORIES, PTOLEMAIC PERIOD, C. 100 BC.)

struggled to throw off the mountain, but his teeth sank into it, and he was unable to see properly. Moses took an axe in his hands, leapt into the air and cut through the giant's ankles. Og crumpled, struck the ground and died. In the Old Testament Book of Deuteronomy, Og was said to be king of Bashan: "Behold, his bedstead was a bedstead of iron . . . nine cubits was the length thereof, and four cubits the breadth of it."

OGDOAD see *NUN*.

OHRMAZD see *AHURA MAZDA*.

OSIRIS, son of the Egyptian deities *GEB* and *NUT*, was originally a god of nature who symbolized the cycle of vegetation. In time, however, he became god of the dead. At his birth, he was pro-

claimed the "Universal Lord", and he grew into a tall and handsome deity. When his father retired, Osiris became king of Egypt and took his sister, *ISIS*, as his queen. He taught humankind how to make bread and wine, and oversaw the building of the first temples and statues to the gods. He also built towns, and laid down just and fair laws. Once Egypt was civilized, Osiris embarked on a great journey, civilizing each country to which he came. His success was largely due to the fact that everyone he encountered was immediately transfixed by his charisma.

When Osiris returned to Egypt many festivals were held in his honour. However, his younger brother, *SETH*, grew jealous of his popularity. He hatched a plan and invited Osiris to a feast, during which a superb coffin was carried in to

them. Feigning innocence, Seth announced that the coffin belonged to whomsoever fitted it. Osiris entered into the joke and lay down in the coffin. Immediately, the lid was nailed down and the coffin thrown into the Nile. The coffin was eventually washed up on the shores of Byblos.

According to another version of the story, Seth killed Osiris after first transforming himself into a crocodile; yet another tale tells how Seth turned himself into a bull and trampled Osiris to death.

When Isis heard what had happened to her husband and brother, she was overcome with grief and began to search for his body. She eventually found it and brought it back to Egypt, where she hid it in a swamp. Seth found the body and cut it into 14 pieces. Undeterred, Isis remade Osiris's body and then

OSIRIS, murdered by Seth and dying, gives his divine sperm, the source of life, to his consort, Isis. (BASALT RELIEF FROM THE SARCOPHAGUS OF NES-SHUTFENE, SAQQARA, 4TH CENTURY BC.)

performed a magic ritual whereby she restored Osiris to life. This was the first rite of embalment. Osiris was by now so disillusioned with his brother that he decided to retire from life and to reign over the dead in the underworld. There, in the court of the underworld, he supervised the judgment of the dead.

Osiris was usually depicted as a bearded man wrapped in mummy bandages and holding a crook and a flail to symbolize his kingship. He symbolizes the regenerative powers of the natural world, as well as the threat posed by severe weather conditions to the well-being of humanity. (See also *UNDERWORLDS; DYING AND RISING GODS*)

P

THE PHARAOHS' (top) treasure chambers were fabled for their unrivalled wealth of gold and magnificent artefacts, and many were rifled in antiquity. This is the treasure chamber of Rhampsinitus.

THE PHARAOH RAMESES II (above) defeated the Khetans in battle. The god-kings were often called to mediate in battle as well as between the gods and the people.

THE PHARAOH RAMESES II (above left) as a young man. Regarded as a divine monarch, the pharaoh was sometimes depicted worshipping his own image. (BAS-RELIEF, 13TH CENTURY BC.)

THE PHARAOH TUTANKHAMEN (right) had a fairly undistinguished reign. However, his tomb at Thebes survived intact throughout the centuries until it was opened in 1922. This golden mask from the inner tomb was amongst the most splendid of the many treasures discovered. (14TH CENTURY BC.)

PAPAS see *ATTIS*.

PHARAOHS ruled over Egypt from around 3100 BC, when the country became unified. In early times, the word pharaoh, meaning "Great House" or "Palace," was never used to refer to the king himself, but under the New Kingdom (c. 1570–1085 BC) the term could be applied directly to the king. Regarded as a divine monarch, the pharaoh was sometimes depicted worshipping his own image, thereby drawing attention to his divine status. He was given the titles of "Horus"; "The Two Ladies" (referring to *NEKHBET* and *WADJET*,

the goddesses of Upper and Lower Egypt); "Horus of Gold"; "King of Upper and Lower Egypt and Lord of the Double Land"; and "Son of Ra and Lord of Diadems". Whenever there was a change of ruler, the queen was said to marry *RA* and to bear a son who became the new king. Pharaohs were often depicted suckling from a goddess to symbolize both their divinity and their relationship to the deity.

According to one papyrus, the wife of a high priest of Ra was made pregnant by the sun god. The ruling pharaoh, Khufu of the fourth dynasty, attempted to prevent the birth, but Ra sent several deities,

led by *ISIS* and *NEPHTHYS*, to look after the woman. The deities delivered and named the children and, before leaving the house, hid three crowns. When the priest found the crowns he realized that his children would become kings.

The pharaoh was responsible for the economic and spiritual welfare of his people, and for the construction and upkeep of the temples. Priests were regarded merely as his representatives. After his death, the pharaoh was believed both to join Ra in his boat which sailed across the sky and to take up kingship in the underworld, as *OSIRIS*. (See also *GATEWAYS TO THE GODS*)

R

PTAH was the god of Memphis, the old capital in the north of Egypt where the *PHAROAHS* were crowned. His priests believed he created the world, although he probably originated as a fertility god. In the third millennium BC, he came to rank third in the divine hierarchy after *AMON* and *RA*.

Believed to be the inventor of the arts, Ptah designed and built secular buildings as well as overseeing the construction of temples, and he was said to have moulded the gods and kings out of metal. In one tradition, he created the world through the power of the word.

Ptah is usually depicted wearing a close-fitting linen wrap and skull cap, and holding the sceptre of dominion. Sometimes, however, he is shown as a twisted, frightening figure, in which guise he was believed to protect humanity from all kinds of evil.

When the power of Memphis declined, Ptah was often associated with other deities, including *OSIRIS*. His consort was the lioness goddess, Sekhmet (see *HATHOR*) and he was the father of Nefertum. The bull *APIS* was worshipped in a temple opposite his and was believed to be an incarnation of the god. (See also *SACRED ANIMALS*)

RA, the supreme manifestation of the sun god of Heliopolis, was a hugely important member of the Egyptian pantheon. He was said to have come into being on the primeval mound that rose out of *NUN* and to have proceeded to plan creation. Sometimes, however, he was depicted as a child rising out of a lotus flower. The Egyptians believed that each day the sun god was born. In the morning, after his bath and breakfast, he began his journey across the sky in his boat

PTAH, the creator god and patron of craftsmen, holds his sceptre of dominion, surmounted by the ankh, or symbol of life.

(*STATUETTE FROM THE TREASURE OF TUTANKHAMEN, 14TH CENTURY BC.*)

RA *(above), the supreme Egyptian sun god, with Aten, another sun god, to the left.* (WALL PAINTING FROM THE TOMB OF SENNEDJEM, THEBES, 13TH CENTURY BC.)

RA *(left), the supreme Egyptian manifestation of the sun god, is usually portrayed as a falcon-headed man wearing the disc of the sun on his head.* (GREAT TEMPLE, ABU SIMBEL.)

and would spend one of the hours of the day inspecting each of his 12 provinces. When the sun went down, Ra was believed to enter the underworld until the morning, when he was born again. All night long, the supreme god had to fight his enemy APEP, the terrible cosmic serpent of the underworld.

Ra gave birth to SHU, the god of air, and Tefnut, the goddess of moisture. According to one myth, the pair disappeared to explore the universe; when Ra finally found them, he was so relieved that he burst into tears. From his tears the first human beings were formed. Another tale tells how, when Ra was an old and dribbling man, the goddess ISIS determined to discover his secret name. She made a snake from earth moistened with the great god's spit and positioned the snake beside a path where the god liked to walk. In due course, the snake bit Ra, poisoning him and causing him such agony that he cried out in pain. Isis agreed to cure him only if he would reveal his name. Ra's suffering was such that he eventually agreed to disclose his secret. Isis promised not to pass on her knowledge to anyone but HORUS and, by speaking the god's true name, healed him.

The PHARAOHS called themselves "Sons of Ra", not only because he was held in great awe but also because he was said to have created order out of chaos. Ra was usually depicted as a falcon wearing a sun disc on his head. (See also MYTHS OF THE FLOOD)

63

DYING AND RISING GODS

STORIES OF BEAUTIFUL AND WELL-LOVED semi-divine youths who died tragically, or were seized by the grim ruler of the underworld but were then miraculously restored to life, echoed through many ancient cultures. Like the promise of a serene afterlife, they raised the possibility that death itself could be conquered. They underlined the regenerative powers of nature, suggesting the continuance of humanity in future generations and, above all, the annual rebirth of the natural world. Dying and rising gods were associated with vegetation, fertility and the harvest: their devotees worshipped them because they needed reassurance that when the summer drought came and food crops died away, they could rely on the resurgence of the next season's growth. Faith in the annual return of a force that could defy death and the powers of darkness gave them confidence that the following year would be fruitful. Fresh green shoots pushing up through the soil can be clearly identified with the eternal youth of these deities rising from the underworld.

ADONIS (above), the beautiful youth, was the lover of Venus, the Roman version of Astarte, goddess of the Phoenicians and Canaanites. He was gored to death by a boar while out hunting and descended to the underworld, but at Venus's entreaty was permitted to return to her for half of each year. On his annual departure from earth, an ecstatic mourning festival was held in the Phoenician city of Byblos, the centre of his cult. (VENUS AND ADONIS BY PYOTR SOLOKOV, CANVAS, 1782.)

WILD ANEMONES (left) forming a red carpet at the foot of Mount Lebanon after the winter rains were said to represent the blood of Tammuz, before his descent to the underworld signalled the beginning of a season of parched earth and withered vegetation. Tammuz, the Mesopotamian god of vegetation, was the consort of the fertility goddess Ishtar. He was consigned by her to spend half the year in the underworld, in recompense for her own release from death.

OSIRIS's (right) death and the story of his grieving widow, Isis, contains elements common to other dying and rising myths. In some versions, Osiris was killed by Seth in the form of a bull or boar; in another he was encased in a coffin which became entwined in a living tree at Byblos, like the myrrh tree from which Adonis was born. Isis breathed new life into Osiris and conceived their son, Horus, but Seth dismembered his body and scattered the pieces, like grain being scattered in a field. Osiris crouches here on a pedestal, flanked by Isis and Horus. (EGYPTIAN GOLD AND LAPIS LAZULI, 9TH CENTURY BC..)

BAAL (left) was the son of the fertility god Dagan. He was armed with thunder (a mace) and lightning (a lance) for his epic battle with the sea god, Yam, who represented the forces of chaos and thus threatened nature. His victory spurred him to challenge the god of death, Mot, but he was killed. He was avenged by his sister and consort Anat, and Mot's defeat restored Baal to life so that fertility could return to the earth.
(SYRIAN LIMESTONE RELIEF, 17TH–13TH CENTURY BC.)

ATTIS (right) was the consort of the Phrygian mother goddess, Cybele. In one version of his myth, he was gored by a wild boar, but according to the most famous story he is said to have castrated himself in a fit of madness brought on by the jealous Cybele. This theme was taken up by adherents of his cult, who mourned his death and celebrated his rebirth in frenzied and bloody rituals each spring.
(MARBLE BUST, IMPERIAL ROME.)

RA-HERARHTY see *HORUS*.

RASHNU was the personification of righteousness and a judge of the dead in ancient Iranian mythology. When people died, their good and bad deeds were weighed in golden scales in order to determine their fate. It took the judges three days and three nights to come to their decision, during which time the soul of the dead person would hover by its body, meditating on its life and anxiously awaiting the verdict. When the judgment had been made, the soul would be sent across the Chinvat, or Cinvat, Bridge, which led to *AHURA MAZDA*'s paradise. A beautiful lady would help the good souls across the bridge. Bad souls would find that the bridge was as narrow and sharp as the edge of a razor and would plunge downwards into the depths where demons waited to inflict every imaginable type of cruelty on them. But the stay in heaven or hell was only temporary, for not until the day of the resurrection will the whole person, body and soul, be judged.

RESEF see *RESHEF*.

RESHEF, or Resef, was the Phoenician god of lightning and plagues. He was referred to as "Lord of the Arrow", probably due to the manner in which he spread disease and sickness all about him. The god could also be invoked for healing. Reshef was sometimes regarded as the consort of the ferocious goddess *ANAT* and was the equivalent of the Mesopotamian plague god, Namtar. The Egyptians assimilated Reshef into their pantheon, where he was regarded as a god of war and depicted brandishing an axe.

RESHEF, the Phoenician god of plagues. From earliest times he was depicted as wielding an axe, or mace and shield, and wearing a tall, pointed headdress. (BRONZE, CANAANITE, LATE BRONZE AGE OR EARLY IRON AGE.)

RUSTEM, the ancient Iranian hero, possessed a magnificent horse, Rakhsh, who was faithful and brave, and assisted him in his battles against dragons and demons.
(ILLUSTRATION FROM SHAH-NAMEH MANUSCRIPT, 1486.)

RUDA, or "Gracious", was a pre-Islamic deity worshipped in northern Arabia. The deity sometimes appears in male form, sometimes female. Usually associated with the evening star, Ruda was sometimes known as Arsu.

RUSTEM, the hero of the 10th-century Iranian epic *Shah-Nameh*, was the son of ZAL, and a nobleman and adviser to the king. Whatever danger threatened the king's realm, Rustem always rode fearlessly into battle: he subdued countless earthly enemies, and fought and conquered demons. On one occasion, a demon surprised Rustem while he was asleep and threw him into the sea; none the less, the hero managed to escape.

Eventually the king, whom Rustem had looked after for countless years, became jealous of him. He ordered his men to dig deep ditches and to line their bases with sharp, upended spears and swords. The king then invited Rustem to go hunting on his land. Although Rustem's horse, Rakhsh, refused to enter the hunting ground, the hero spurred him onwards. Both horse and rider fell into a ditch and were pierced through and through. Rustem died, but before doing so, he shot the king dead with his bow and arrow. Rustem's bravery symbolized the battles between the Persians and the Turanians, Indians and Semites. (See also HEROES AND QUESTS)

SAHAR AND SALEM see SHACHAR AND SHALIM.

SANDA see SANTAS.

SANTAS was an ancient god of western Asia Minor. He was often associated with the mother goddess KUBABA and was sometimes referred to as "King". Santas sometimes appeared as the Babylonian god MARDUK, and he was assimilated into the Greek pantheon as the god Sandon.

SAOSHYANT is the name of the final saviour in Iranian mythology. His appearance will signal the arrival of the last days and the coming of Frashkart, the "final renewal". It is sometimes said that Saoshyant will be born of a virgin, who will become impregnated by the preserved seed of ZOROASTER while bathing in a lake. According to one tradition, the cycle of the world is made up of four ages, each lasting 3,000 years. The first 3,000 years were those of spiritual creation during which AHURA MAZDA brought the benign spirits and the FRAVASHIS, the guardian angels, into being. In the second 3,000 years, Ahura Mazda created the material world, GAYOMART, the primeval man, and GEUSH URVAN the primeval bull, although his work was hindered by ANGRA MAINYU, who introduced evil and destruction. In the third age, good and evil were locked in an intense struggle with one another and Angra Mainyu filled the world with evil spirits. At the beginning of the fourth and final period – the present age – the religious reformer Zoroaster appeared. This last age is that of Saoshyant, the saviour who will finally appear in order to renew the world and resurrect the dead.

A flood of molten metal will submerge and purify the whole planet, and Angra Mainyu will finally be destroyed. During the final renewal itself, the whole of humanity will be subjected to a burning torrent, which will cleanse them of all their evil ways and thus allow them to live with Ahura Mazda. Those who have lived blameless lives will experience the scalding torrent as no more than "warm milk". According to one tradition, Saoshyant will sacrifice a bull and mix its fat with the magical elixir, HAOMA, thereby creating a drink of immortality, which he will give to all humanity.

RUSTEM was surprised while sleeping by the demon Akwan, who tried to hurl him into the sea. Needless to say, the hero managed to escape. (ILLUSTRATION FROM SHAH-NAMEH, LITHOGRAPH.)

.IVDA SCARIOTO

.LVCIFERO.

SATAN *or Lucifer, the fallen angel, came to be seen as the ruler of hell. Here, with a triple face, he devours the traitor Judas Iscariot and two other sinners. (HAND-COLOURED WOODCUT, 1512.)*

SATAN, whose name means the "Adversary", plays a minor role in the Old Testament as the opponent of humankind, ordered by YAHWEH to test humanity's faith. He is an angel in the kingdom of heaven and deals directly with Yahweh.

In the Book of Job, Yahweh instructs Satan to destroy Job's family and possessions and cover him with boils, with the intention of tempting him into cursing God. However, the patient Job declares: "What? Shall we receive good at the hand of God, and shall we not receive evil? In all this did not Job sin with his lips."

Satan came to be viewed by the Hebrews as the supreme evil being, under whom was ranged a hierarchy of demons. In opposition to the demons were the angels. Thus, the Hebrews came to see creation as a battle between the forces of good and evil, suggesting the influence of Persian thinking.

One tale relates how Satan, the devil and "prince of this world", rebelled against Yahweh and was hurled by an angel into the abyss. He is imagined in the form of a snake or a dragon. In Christianity, Satan became the embodiment of evil. He was pictured as a handsome man with horns, a pointed tail and cloven hoofs.

In the apocryphal Book of John the Evangelist, Jesus describes Satan's transformation: "My Father changed his appearance because of his pride, and the light was taken from him, and his face became unto a heated iron, and his face became wholly like that of a man: and he drew with his tail the third part of the angels of God and was cast out from the seat of God and the stewardship of the heavens." (See also ANGELS AND DJINN)

SEBEK, or Sobek, the Egyptian crocodile god, was represented either as the reptile itself or as a man with a crocodile's head. Sebek's following was greatest at Crocodilopolis, capital of the province of Fayum. A live crocodile called Petsuchos, said to be an incarnation of the god, was kept in a lake attached to Sebek's main sanctuary. Sebek's devotees sought the god's protection by drinking water from the pool and feeding the crocodile on delicacies. In the 13th dynasty, during the second millennium BC, many of the kings were called Sebekhotep, or "Sebek is Satisfied", and it is thought that many people regarded the god as the chief deity. According to some stories, the evil god SETH hid himself in Sebek's body to escape being punished for murdering OSIRIS.

Sebek was sometimes regarded as the son of NEITH, the great mother and warrior goddess, who was also credited with having given birth to the terrifying snake APEP. (See also SACRED ANIMALS)

SEKHMET see HATHOR.

SETH, an Egyptian god of storms and chaos, came to signify evil, although he was widely held in high esteem. The son of the earth god GEB and sky goddess NUT, he was rough and wild, with red hair and white skin.

Seth became so jealous of his gracious elder brother, OSIRIS, that he murdered him and appointed himself king of Egypt. However, unknown to Seth, Osiris and ISIS had conceived a child, HORUS. Isis nursed Horus in secret until he was old enough to avenge his father, and Osiris himself occasionally returned from the underworld to

SEBEK *embodied the deadly power of the crocodile against its prey, and epitomized the military might of the pharoah. (RELIEF FROM TEMPLE OF SEBEK AND HORUS, KOM OMBO.)*

SETH (above), the slayer of Osiris, was not always considered evil. He was worshipped in prehistoric times, and again by the Ramessid pharaohs.

SETH (left), god of evil and the desert, with his wife Nephthys, the sister of Isis. He is depicted as a brutish animal, part pig, part ass. *(BASALT SCULPTURE.)*

tells how the god came upon *HATHOR*, the cow goddess, when she was bathing in a river and raped her. Seth was immediately struck down with a terrible illness and his wife, Anat, appealed to Ra for help. Eventually Isis helped Anat cure Seth. The god symbolizes the harsh aspects of the natural world and was said to live in the arid desert.

SHACHAR AND SHALIM, or Shar and Shalim, "Dawn" and "Dusk", were the offspring of *EL*, the supreme god of the Phoenician pantheon. They were also known as Sahar and Salem. In ancient texts discovered at Ras Shamra in Syria, on the site of the city of Ugarit, the deities are described as having been conceived when El stretched out his hands like waves to the sea, making his two wives fruitful. The two wives are generally believed to be Ashera (see *ASTARTE*) and *ANAT*.

instruct his son in the art of war. When the right moment arrived, Horus went into battle against Seth and overcame him.

Before a divine tribunal, Seth declared that he was entitled to the throne of Egypt because he was the only deity strong and brave enough to protect *RA*. Although some of the gods sided with Seth, Isis per-suaded them to change their minds. When Osiris was consulted in the underworld, he demanded to know why his son had not been allowed to take his rightful place on the throne and threatened to send demons to attack the gods. Ra finally agreed to Horus's claim.

According to one story, Seth went to live with Ra in the sky. Another version of the myth tells how Seth was condemned to carry Osiris on his shoulders for all eternity. Yet another tale relates how the goddess *NEITH* suggested that Seth should be given two foreign goddesses, *ANAT* and *ASTARTE*, as his wives, in order to console him for having lost the throne to Horus. A tale concerning Seth and Anat

SHAMASH was the Babylonian sun god, able to expose injustice and falsehood with his searching rays. He was also the god of divination, and could be consulted through a soothsayer. He is shown here in his emanation as Mrn, chief deity of the city of Hatra. (PARTHIAN SCULPTURE, C. AD 150-200.)

SHU, the Egyptian god of air, was the male half of the first divine couple. His name is sometimes translated as "Emptiness", sometimes as "He Who Holds Up". Shu was created when the supreme god RA, as Ra-Atum, spat or sneezed him out of his mouth. His consort was Tefnut, goddess of moisture, who was created in the same fashion. Shu and Tefnut left Ra-Atum to explore NUN, the dark abyss that existed at the very beginning of time. Ra-Atum was distraught, thinking he had lost his children. When they returned, he wept tears of joy, from which the first human beings were formed.

Shu and Tefnut begat GEB, the earth, and NUT, the sky. Eventually, Shu separated his two children by pushing Nut upwards with his arms. He is often depicted as supporting the sky.

Shu succeeded Ra to the throne, but the followers of the terrifying snake APEP continually attacked him and, growing tired of the ceaseless conflict, Shu abdicated, leaving his son Geb to become king. After a terrible storm lasting more than a week, Shu took up residence in the sky. Sometimes, as son of the sun god, Ra, Shu is represented with the head of a lion.

SHAMASH was the Babylonian god of the sun, who saw all things and thus also came to be regarded as a god of justice and divination. Known to the Sumerians as Utu, his light uncovered every misdeed and enabled him to see into the future. Each morning, the scorpion men opened a gate in the vast mountain of Mashu and Shamash made his way out into the sky. Slowly, he climbed the mountain until he reached the high point of the sky; as evening approached, he rode his chariot towards another great mountain and disappeared through its gates. During the night, Shamash journeyed through the depths of the earth until he reached the first gate once more. The sun god's consort was Aya, who gave birth to Kittu, justice, and Misharu, law and righteousness. Shamash was depicted seated on a throne.

SHAR AND SHALIM see *SHACHAR AND SHALIM*.

SHAUSHKA was an important Hurrian deity who was identified with ISHTAR, the Babylonian goddess of love, fertility and war. Like Ishtar, she was depicted as a winged figure standing on a lion, and was attended by two women. The goddess seems to have had a dual nature.

SIN, the Sumerian-Babylonian moon god, was the father of SHAMASH, the sun god, INANA (or ISHTAR), the planet Venus, and Nusku, the god of fire. Sometimes known as Suen, or Nanna, he was conceived when the air god ENLIL raped the grain goddess NINLIL and was born in the underworld. Sin's consort was Ningal, or the "Great Lady". Sin was usually depicted as an old man with a blue beard, and he was called the "Shining Boat of Heaven". Every evening, he would climb into his crescent-shaped boat and sail across the skies. Sometimes, the crescent moon was regarded as the god's weapon and the full moon as his crown.

Sin was the enemy of the wicked, for his light revealed their evil ways. On one occasion, the utukku, or evil genies, hatched a plot against Sin and, with the help of Shamash, Ishtar, the goddess of love and fertility, and *ADAD*, the god of thunder, they eclipsed his light. However, the great god *MARDUK* waged war against the conspirators and gave Sin back his radiance.

Sin was also held to be wise and was believed to measure time with his waxing and waning. Moreover, by raising the marsh waters around the city of Ur, where his temple stood, he ensured the well-being of cattle by enabling them to enjoy an abundant supply of food. (See also *GATEWAYS TO THE GODS*)

SIYAMEK see *HAOSHYANGHA*.

SOBEK see *SEBEK*.

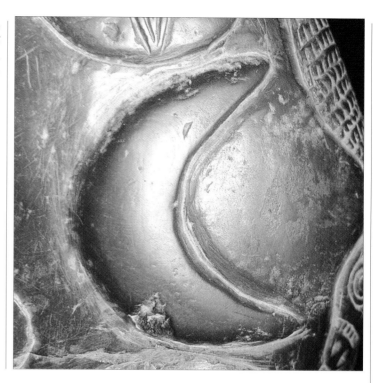

SIN (right) was the Babylonian moon god, whose symbol, the crescent moon, is depicted on this carved stone. The god was held in supreme regard in Mesopotamia. His chief cult centres were at Ur and Harran. (KUDURRU, C. 1120 BC.)

SHU (below), supports a head-rest found in the tomb of Tutankhamen. The god of air, Shu was the father of the sky goddess, Nut, and was often depicted in this position, supporting the sky above his head. (CARVED IVORY, 14TH CENTURY BC..)

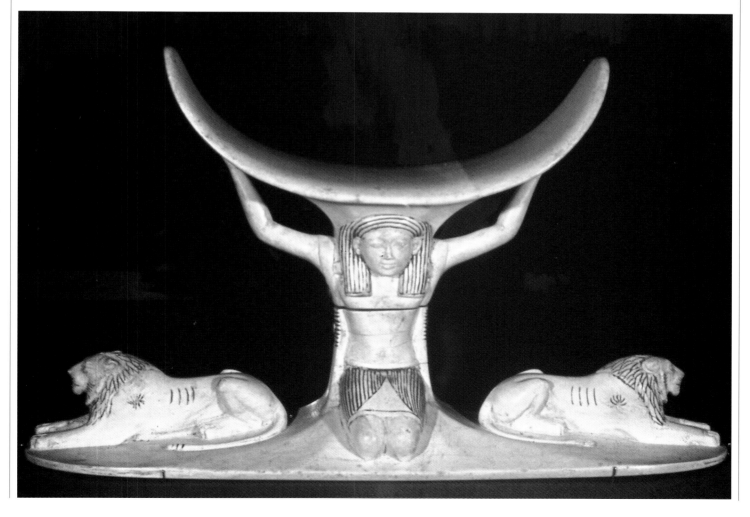

SOLOMON

SOLOMON was the Old Testament king who ruled over Israel in the tenth century BC. He was noted for his great wisdom and for building *YAHWEH*'s marvellous temple at Jerusalem. Under the influence of his many foreign wives, Solomon also built shrines for other gods, thereby incurring Yahweh's wrath. Solomon's seal, a six-sided star, became an important symbol used as an amulet or talisman. According to Arabic mythology, the star and the real name of God were etched on King Solomon's magic ring, thereby enabling him to command armies of demons. (See also *ANGELS AND DJINN*)

SPENTA ARMAITI is one of the *AMESA SPENTAS*, or the "Holy Immortals", of ancient Iranian mythology. Like the other Amesa Spentas, she is believed to have originated before the religious reforms of *ZOROASTER* and to have been assimilated into the purified religion as an aspect of *AHURA MAZDA*, the supreme being. Spenta Armaiti was patroness of the earth, and symbolized submission and devotion. She was widely believed to be the spiritual mother of all human beings, and people were taught to say, "My mother is Spendarmat, Archangel of the Earth, and my father is Ohrmazd, the Lord Wisdom."

According to one tradition, she was the mother of *GAYOMART*, the primordial being. As Gayomart lay dying, his body separated into seven metals. Spenta Armaiti gathered together the gold and grew a plant from it. From this plant came the first human couple.

The name Spenta Armaiti is sometimes translated as "Wisdom" or "Devotion".

SRAOSHA was known as the "Ear" of *AHURA MAZDA*, the principle of good in ancient Iranian mythology. He was one of the *YAZATAS*, Zoroastrianism's "Beings Worthy of Worship". As the "Ear" of Ahura Mazda, he was the means by which those who worshipped the supreme being could gain access to him. During the night, Sraosha guarded the whole of creation from evil demons.

SUEN see *SIN*.

TAHMURAS, according to ancient Iranian mythology, was the son of *HAOSHYANGHA*, the first king. He taught people how to spin and weave, and how to train birds of prey. On one occasion, he succeeded in capturing *ANGRA MAINYU* and, after leaping on to his back, forced the evil being to carry him on a tour of the world. However, while Tahmuras was away on his travels, the *DAEVAS* began to create havoc, so Tahmuras had to return and take up arms against them.

The daevas gathered together a noisy army, which hid itself in thick black smoke. Undeterred by this, Tahmuras captured two-thirds of the aggressors with the help of his magic arts and struck down the remainder with his massive club. The daevas pleaded for mercy and promised Tahmuras that if he spared their lives, they would teach him a marvellous secret. Tahmuras relented and, in return, the daevas taught him how to write and made him extremely wise and learned.

TAMMUZ, the Babylonian god of vegetation and the harvest, was a dying and rising god. Relatively low in standing among the gods, he was nevertheless extremely popular with the people and had a widespread following. His marriage to *ISHTAR*, the lustful goddess of love and fertility, led to his death: just as corn is cut down suddenly at the height of its splendour, so Tammuz was forced to retire to the underworld. Ishtar was devastated at his loss and underwent a period of wailing and lamentation. Each year after the harvest, those who worshipped Ishtar and Tammuz took part in a mourning ritual.

Ishtar eventually sought out Tammuz in the underworld and managed to secure his release, on condition that he return to the underworld for half of each year. Tammuz returned to the land of the living and took up his position at the gate of the sky god, *ANU*. It was there that the wise man *ADAPA* encountered him, when Adapa was summoned before Anu for demonstrating too much power. Adapa flattered Tammuz, who rewarded him by interceding on his behalf.

Tammuz's sister was Belili. In Sumerian myth, he was known as *DUMUZI*, the consort of *INANA*. (See also *DYING AND RISING GODS*)

ⲤⲞⲖⲞⲘⲰⲚ

HEROES AND QUESTS

MYTHS ABOUT MORTAL HEROES HAVE AN immediacy that comes from their recognizable human characteristics. Though the great heroes performed astonishing acts of bravery and achieved feats that were far beyond the capability of any real man, their adventures took place on earth and, in some ways, they behaved as other men did – falling in love, falling asleep, making friends, making mistakes – so that those who listened to their stories could identify with them as they could not with remote gods and goddesses. These men feared death and could not avoid it, hard as they tried. A perilous journey was usually central to the hero's story. There were many thrilling adventures on the way, with twists and turns that diverted him from his path, and selfless deeds such as killing monsters that frustrated him in his quest but saved the day for ordinary folk.

GILGAMESH (above), king of Uruk, or Erech, was the hero of a number of Sumerian stories that were combined and written down by Babylonian scribes in about 2000 BC. Gilgamesh was said to be two-thirds god and one-third man because his mother was the goddess Ninsun. From her he derived his great strength. Despite his heroic stature, he began his reign as a tyrannical king, whose people were eventually driven to call on the gods for help in subduing him. (ASSYRIAN CYLINDER SEAL IMPRESSION, 1350–1000 BC.)

ENKIDU (above left) was a wild man sent by the gods to deal with Gilgamesh, in answer to his people's prayers. He was, however, even more unruly than the king. Gilgamesh conceived a plan to civilize Enkidu. As a test of strength, they fought in a great wrestling match, but neither could outdo the other, and the two became friends. Their adventures together included the killing of fierce bulls and the fire-breathing demon Humbaba. (AKKADIAN CYLINDER SEAL IMPRESSION, c. 2300 BC.)

GILGAMESH (left) resisted the seductive advances of the goddess Ishtar. Incensed, she sent the bull of heaven to avenge her honour, but with Enkidu's help, Gilgamesh managed to stab the bull. The gods were outraged and decided that Enkidu must pay for his part in the exploit. Within a few days, he had fallen ill and died. The loss of his friend instilled the fear of death in Gilgamesh and he embarked on a quest to find eternal life. (ILLUSTRATION BY E. WALLCOUSINS FROM MYTHS OF BABYLONIA AND ASSYRIA BY DONALD MACKENZIE.)

USHANABI (above), the ferryman, was the only man who knew how to cross the treacherous waters of death safely. He guided Gilgamesh over them on his way to reach the old man Utnapishtim, the sole survivor of the great flood, who had been granted immortality by the gods. Gilgamesh hoped that Utnapishtim would be able to tell him the secret of eternal life. (ILLUSTRATION FROM GILGAMESH BY ZABELLE C BOYAJIAN, 1924.)

UTNAPISHTIM (above) reluctantly told Gilgamesh of a plant growing at the bottom of the sea which had the power to give him eternal youth. Gilgamesh found the plant, but as he bent to pick it, a serpent smelt it and stole it. In this way, snakes acquired the ability to stay young forever by simply shedding their ageing skin. Gilgamesh was forced to understand that his death was inevitable and returned to his kingdom. (ILLUSTRATION FROM GILGAMESH BY ZABELLE C BOYAJIAN, 1924.)

RUSTEM (left), alone of all men, dared to fight the great White Demon in order to free the king, who had been inspired by the evil Angra Mainyu to try to usurp the throne of the ruler of Mazinderan. Rustem found the demon sleeping in his mountain lair, woke him and wrestled with him until "blood and sweat ran down in rivers from their bodies." Rustem was victorious and cut off the demon's head. (ILLUSTRATION FROM SHAH-NAMEH, LITHOGRAPH.)

RUSTEM (above), the Iranian hero, was born in a mysterious fashion, as a result of the incantations of a wizard and with the help of the magical feathers of the Simurgh bird. He was as tall as eight normal men and was famed for his strength and prowess in battle. One of his exploits in his youth was the killing of a rogue white elephant with a blow from an ox-headed mace. (ILLUSTRATION FROM SHAH-NAMEH BY SHIRAZ, C. 1545.)

RUSTEM (left) searched the country for a horse and eventually caught one that had in fact been set aside for him from birth. Rakhsh was as magnificent and brave as the hero himself, with the strength of an elephant and the speed of a racing camel. On one occasion, when Rustem was sleeping and unarmed, his horse saved his life by killing a lion before it could attack him. (ILLUSTRATION FROM SHAH-NAMEH BY INJU SHIRAZ, 1341.)

TARU, the Hittite weather god, was the father of *TELEPINU*. Like many other myths originating in West Asia, those featuring Taru are concerned with the annual cycle of vegetation. The tales relate his battles against a terrible monster, the giant serpent or dragon *ILLUYANKAS*. When Taru overcame the monster, vegetation flourished, but when he was vanquished all plant life withered and died.

According to one tale, Illuyankas managed to defeat the weather god. However, the goddess *INARAS* then hatched a plot whereby she managed to trap the terrible monster. The goddess prepared an enormous banquet and invited Illuyankas and his numerous offspring to come and join her in feasting.

When they had eaten their fill, the monsters discovered that they were too fat to fit through the tunnel that led to their underground home. The hero *HUPASIYAS*, Inaras's human consort, then tied the monsters up with a rope, whereupon Taru, assisted by the other gods, overcame them.

According to another version of the myth, the serpent overcame Taru, and seized his heart and eyes. Taru then fathered a son whom he married to the daughter of Illuyankas. The son asked for his father's missing organs as a dowry

payment and returned them to Taru. The weather god then slew Illuyankas in a terrifying sea battle. He also killed his son, probably in revenge for his having sided with the monster during the battle.

TEFNUT see *SHU*.

TELEPINU was a Hittite god of agriculture who controlled the fertility of plants and animals. His father, *TARU*, the weather god, said of him: "This son of mine is mighty; he harrows and ploughs, he irrigates the fields and makes the crops grow."

On one famous occasion, which has become known as the "myth of the disappearing god", Telepinu suddenly vanished; his haste was such that he put his boots on the wrong feet. Immediately, all life on earth began to wither and die. Even the gods began to starve. Fire was extinguished, animals perished, the trees lost their leaves, and the fields became dry and parched. "Barley and emmer wheat throve no more, oxen, sheep and humans ceased to conceive, and those who were pregnant could not bear." The sun threw an enormous feast for the gods, but his guests were unable to eat their fill or quench their thirst. Finally Taru explained that his son was angry and had disappeared, taking all good things with him.

TESHUB (above) god of the tempest and head of the Hittite pantheon, bears an axe and a three-pronged lightning fork. He was also a god of battle and overcame Kumarbi, the father of the gods. Kumarbi's son Ullikummi fought to take control of Teshub's city, but without success.

THOTH (below), the Egyptian moon god and vizier of Osiris, records the result of the weighing of a heart. As Osiris' sacred scribe, he was associated with secret knowledge and helped at the burial of Osiris. (FROM THE BOOK OF THE DEAD OF HUNEFER, C. 1310 BC.)

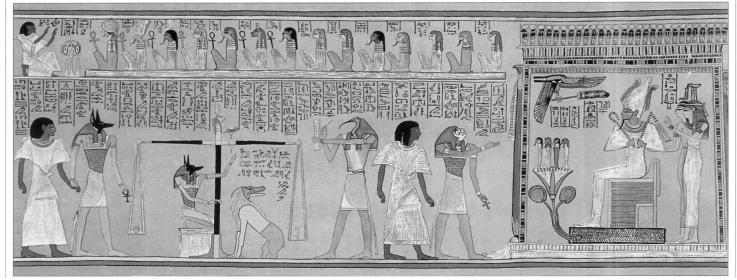

All the gods, both great and small, proceeded to search for Telepinu. The sun sent out the eagle saying, "Go, search the high mountains, search the hollow valleys, search the dark-blue waters." However, although the eagle explored the entire country, he failed to find the missing god. Then, the weather god asked the mother goddess, HANNAHANNA, for advice. Hannahanna told the weather god to go himself and look for Telepinu, but Taru soon gave up and sat down to rest. Then Hannahanna suggested sending a bee to look for the god. Although the weather god objected, the goddess ignored him and told the bee to find the Telepinu, sting him on his hands and feet to wake him up, and then bring him back home.

At length, the bee found Telepinu asleep in a field. When the bee stung him, the god fell into such a frenzy that he proceeded to cause yet more devastation, killing human beings, oxen and sheep in his wake.

Eventually, the goddess Kamrusepas managed to calm him down using her magic spells: "She stilled his anger, she stilled his wrath, she stilled his rage, she stilled his fury." Telepinu flew home on the back of an eagle, and life returned to normal: "He released the embers of the hearth, he released the sheep in the fold, he released the oxen in the stall. The mother attended to her child, the ewe attended to her lamb, the cow attended to her calf."

TESHUB was a god of the tempest who was worshipped throughout western Asia. He is believed to have originated among the Hurrians, although the chief myth concerning his activities has been passed down by the Hittites. In the Hittite mythological texts, it is recorded how the fearsome god Teshub overcame KUMARBI, the father of the gods. Kumarbi

fathered a son, ULLIKUMMI, who was made of diorite stone and grew to a huge size on the back of the giant, Upelluri. In order to view the vast creature, Teshub climbed to the summit of a high mountain. On seeing the monster, the terrified weather god persuaded the other deities to join him in launching an attack. However, their assault proved unsuccessful. Ullikummi succeeded in advancing as far as the gates of Teshub's city, whereupon he forced the god to abdicate his throne.

Teshub sought advice from the wise god EA who, after pondering a while, unearthed the ancient saw with which heaven and earth had been divided, and used the tool to sever the diorite stone at its feet. As a result, Ullikummi's power quickly faded, whereupon the gods decided to renew their attack on him. Although the end of the myth is missing, it is generally believed that Teshub eventually regained his kingdom and throne.

Teshub was the husband of HEPAT, who was often given almost equal standing with her husband, and sometimes took precedence over him. Teshub's attributes were an axe and lightning flashes, and he was sometimes depicted as a bearded figure, holding a club, with his feet resting on mountain deities. His chariot was drawn by two bulls.

THOTH, the Egyptian moon god, presided over scribes and knowledge, and was "Lord of the Sacred Words". He was sometimes said to be the sun god RA's eldest son, although, according to one tradition, he sprang from the head of the evil god, SETH.

Thoth is usually regarded as the vizier of OSIRIS, god of vegetation and the dead, as well as his sacred scribe. Because he was associated with secret knowledge, Thoth was able to help at the burial of Osiris. He also helped to look after HORUS when ISIS was bringing him up.

Eventually, Thoth succeeded Horus to the throne of Egypt and reigned peacefully over the land for more than 3,000 years. Afterwards, he took his place in the sky as the moon.

According to one story, he was ordered by Ra to light up the sky at night. There, he was slowly devoured by monsters who were, however, repeatedly forced to disgorge him bit by bit. Thoth was usually depicted as an ibis or as a baboon. It was said that Thoth

wrote a book of magic, known as the *Book of Thoth*, which lies buried in a tomb near Memphis. The spells within the book were said to give the user power over the gods. Thoth was also said to record the verdict of the judgment of the dead in the underworld. (See also *SACRED ANIMALS*)

THOTH, god of the moon, writing and knowledge, with a scribe. Thoth was often depicted as a baboon, one of his sacred animals. (BRONZE, ARMARNA, C. 1340 BC.)

useful plants. It was said that he helped *AHURA MAZDA*, the principle of goodness, in his struggle against every evil.

TISTRIYN see *TISHTRYA*.

ULLIKUMMI was the son of *KUMARBI*, originally an ancient Anatolian deity who was later introduced into Hittite mythology. The myth of Ullikummi concerns Kumarbi's attempt to wreak vengeance on his first son, *TESHUB*, who had overthrown him.

Kumarbi nursed the thought of creating an evil being and eventually slept with a vast stone, which subsequently gave birth to a son, Ullikummi. The boy was made of diorite stone, and in order that he might grow up in safety the deities placed him on the shoulders of the giant Upelluri in the middle of the sea. The child rapidly grew bigger and bigger until the water reached no higher than his middle, at which point the sun god noticed him and immediately told Teshub of the impending threat. Teshub wept

TIAMAT, according to Mesopotamian mythology, was the turbulent, salt-water ocean that existed at the beginning of time. The universal primeval mother, she was depicted as a monstrous female dragon and was believed to embody the forces of chaos. The waters of Tiamat mingled with the fresh-water primordial ocean, *APSU*, and, in doing so, initiated the creation of the gods.

In time, Apsu grew tired of the clamour of the gods and began to plot their destruction. Tiamat at first refused to take part in Apsu's plan, but when the water god *EA* captured both Apsu and Mummu, the waves, Tiamat was spurred into action. After giving birth to an army of monsters, "sharp of tooth and merciless of fang", she marched against Ea and the other gods.

For some time, all attempts to subdue Tiamat failed until finally *MARDUK*, Ea's son, was chosen to confront her. Tiamat opened her jaws to swallow Marduk, but the god threw a raging storm into her mouth so that she was unable to close it. Marduk then caught Tiamat in a net and, after piercing her with an arrow, tore her innards apart. After slaughtering Tiamat's army of monsters, Marduk split Tiamat's skull and slashed her body in two. From one half of her body, he made the vault of the heavens, from the other half, the floor of the ocean. Then Marduk pierced Tiamat's eyes to form the sources of the rivers Tigris and Euphrates and bent her tail up into the sky to make the Milky Way. (See also *SERPENTS AND DRAGONS*)

TISHTRYA, or Tistriyn, was the name given by the ancient Iranians to the dog star. He was regarded as the god of water, whether that of the clouds, lakes, rivers or seas. Tishtrya also provided the seeds of

with fear but, after being comforted by his sister, resolved to attack the monstrous being. However, though Teshub summoned the thunder and rain to help him, he was unable to defeat the creature.

Before long, Ullikummi had reached the gates of Teshub's city and forced the weather god to abdicate. Distraught, Teshub sought help from the wise god EA, who retrieved a saw that had originally been used to separate heaven from earth. Ea sliced through Ullikummi's ankles, and the monster's power

UTNAPISHTIM was told by Ea to build a boat and take every kind of living thing aboard. The gods were about to punish the wicked city of Shurripak with a deluge, but Ea wished Utnapishtim to survive. (ILLUSTRATION FROM GILGAMESH BY ZABELLE C BOYAJIAN, 1924.)

faded. The gods then renewed their attack on Ullikummi, and Teshub regained the throne.

UTNAPISHTIM, according to one version of the Mesopotamian flood myth, was the wise man who alone survived the flood. The gods ANU, ENLIL, NINURTA and Ennugi decided to destroy humankind, having grown tired of their ways. However, EA, the water god, warned Utnapishtim of the conspiracy, and told him to build a boat and in it store the seeds of all life. Utnapishtim built a huge vessel 120 cubits high and loaded it with his family, his cattle and numerous other animals and birds.

On the evening that he finished his work, a filthy rain began to fall, and everyone on earth was stricken with terror. For six days and six

nights, the deluge continued until, at daybreak on the seventh day, it suddenly ceased and all that was left of humanity was a vast heap of thick mud.

Utnapishtim, whose marvellous boat had come to the rest on the summit of Mount Nisir, cried out in grief. He let loose one bird after another from his boat, but they all returned, having found nowhere they could alight. However, when at last Utnapishtim released a raven, it failed to return, signifying that it must have found dry land.

In gratitude to the gods, Utnapishtim placed offerings to them on the summit of the mountain. Enlil, however, was furious to see that a human being had escaped the wrath of the gods. Ea eventually managed to calm Enlil down, whereupon Enlil took

Utnapishtim and his wife by the hand and said that from now on they would be immortal, like the gods themselves.

Some time after these events, the hero GILGAMESH, a descendent of Utnapishtim, sought out the immortal in the hope of learning the secret of eternal life from him. Utnapishtim refused to disclose the secret, but nonetheless directed Gilgamesh to the bottom of the sea to find the plant of rejuvenation. Unfortunately, on Gilgamesh's journey home, it was stolen from him by a serpent when the hero stopped to bathe and rest. (See also MYTHS OF THE FLOOD; HEROES AND QUESTS)

UTTUKU see SIN.

UTU see SHAMASH.

W

VOHU MANO was one of the *AMESA SPENTAS*, or "Holy Immortals", of ancient Iranian mythology. These divine beings were believed to people the universe and to look after humanity. They are thought to have been worshipped before the time of the religious reformer *ZOROASTER*. Although Zoroaster denounced the old gods, he continued to venerate the Amesa Spentas as aspects of *AHURA MAZDA*, the one true spirit set in opposition to *ANGRA MAINYU*, the spirit of darkness. It was said that when Zoroaster was about 30 years old, Vohu Mano transported his spirit to Ahura Mazda, thereby bringing about his spiritual enlightenment. Vohu Mano ("Good Thought" or "Spirit of Good") reigned over useful animals and was often represented by the cow.

WADD was a moon god worshipped in certain parts of southern Arabia from the fifth to second centuries BC. His name means "Love" or "Friendship", and his sacred animal was the snake. Wadd is

VOHU MANU, the "Good Thought", was one of the Amesa Spentas of Iranian mythology. He personified the wisdom of Ahura Mazda, portrayed here presenting the crown of the kingdom of Persia to Ardechir I. (ROCK CARVING, EARLY 3RD CENTURY BC.)

referred to in the Qur'an as a pagan divinity, one of five idols erected by the descendants of Cain.

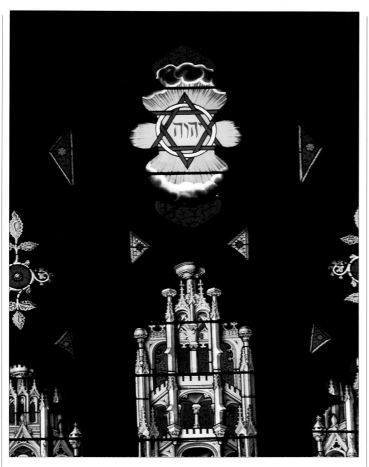

WADJET was the cobra goddess of Lower Egypt. She was usually represented as a cobra about to strike, although she sometimes appeared as a lioness. In the myth that relates how ISIS brought up her child HORUS in secret, Wadjet appears as the young god's nurse. Both Wadjet and NEKHBET were believed to protect the PHARAOH. (See also SACRED ANIMALS)

YAHWEH, or Jahweh, was regarded by the tribes of Israel as the creator of all things and the judge of all nations. He probably originated as a mountain god and was identified with EL, the supreme deity of the Canaanite pantheon. Yahweh intervened in earthly affairs, often through his prophets. He demanded that his followers should worship no other deity and was a jealous god. Though he dealt severely with anyone who strayed from his teachings, he was a god of

YAHWEH's followers avoided pronouncing the four Hebrew letters that made up his name, considering it too sacred to be pronounced aloud.

righteousness and ultimately merciful. No physical likeness was ever attributed to him.

The Third Commandment decrees, "Thou shalt not take the name of the Lord thy God in vain", so his followers avoided pronouncing the four Hebrew letters, YHWH or JHWH, which made up his name. The letters are supposed to represent the identity of God and are usually interpreted as meaning "I am that I am". From the 13th century, Yahweh was sometimes known in English as Jehovah. (See also SERPENTS AND DRAGONS; ANGELS AND DJINN)

YAM, or Yamm, or Jamm, was the Phoenician god of the sea and water in general. One of his titles

was "Ruler River". According to one myth, Yam asked the supreme god, EL, to grant him power over the other gods. El agreed but warned him that he must first conquer BAAL.

The fertility god equipped himself with magical weapons made by the smith gods and went into battle. He succeeded in killing Yam, proceeded to scatter his remains and then crowned himself king. The myth symbolizes the chaotic forces of nature being overcome by its civilizing aspect, which ensures the fertility of the crops.

Another tale tells how Yam was compensated for his defeat by being given the goddess ASTARTE as his bride. Yam was sometimes referred to as a dragon or serpent, or as the sea monster, LEVIATHAN.

YAMM see YAM.

THE YAZATAS, or "Beings Worthy of Worship", were the protective spirits of Zoroastrianism. Most of them were ancient Iranian gods who were incorporated into ZOROASTER's reformed religion as helpers of the supreme being, AHURA MAZDA. Some of the Yazatas corresponded to the stars and planets, others to the elements, while many embodied abstract concepts. Sometimes, the celestial Yazatas were said to be led by Ahura Mazda and the terrestrial Yazatas by Zoroaster. They included in their number RASHNU and SRAOSHA.

YAM, the Phoenician sea god, represented the turbulence of nature. He was defeated by the fertility god, Baal. In some versions of his myth he married the goddess Astarte, though she is more often described as the consort of Baal himself. (GILDED BRONZE, 19TH–18TH CENTURY BC.)

ANGELS AND DJINN

ANGELS ARE INTERMEDIARIES BETWEEN heaven and earth, sent to bring messages to humankind – their name comes from the Greek word for "messenger". The Hebrew patriarch Jacob had a vision of angels on foot, ascending and descending a ladder which stood on the earth and reached up to heaven. Later concepts of heaven were of a more remote realm, from which winged angels flew down to earth. Angels are mentioned frequently in the

Bible, praising Yahweh or appearing to humans bearing announcements or instructions from him. Islamic angels are also winged messengers; another of their tasks is to record the good and bad deeds of men, and they examine the faith of the dead on their first night in the grave. Djinn are less predictable. Originally nature spirits, they are a disruptive influence on humankind, capable of causing madness. A sinful man risks being turned into a djinnee (a lesser djinn) after his death.

THE PROTECTIVE SPIRITS (above) of ancient Iranian mythology were portrayed as winged creatures, and it was perhaps this imagery that influenced the development of the idea of angels' wings. Protective, sheltering wings were an important symbol of the beneficence of Ahura Mazda, the supreme god of the Iranians, and are used to represent him. (PERSIAN MINIATURE, C. 1370–80.)

THE DJINN (above) were ugly and evil supernatural beings in pre-Islamic times, the fiery spirits of wild, desolate places who exercised their malign powers under a cloak of invisibility or by changing their shape at will. Their name means "furious" or "possessed". Though they were capable of redemption under Islam, those who refused to acknowledge Allah became demons. (SYRIAN RELIEF SCULPTURE, 9TH CENTURY BC.)

THE ANGELS (left), who were created before human beings, objected to Allah's plan to populate the earth, on the grounds that humanity would rebel against him. However, when Allah created Adam as the first prophet and taught him the names of all things, all the angels agreed to bow down before him. The single exception was Iblis, the devil, who considered that as he was born of fire he was superior to a being made of earth. (OTTOMAN MINIATURE, 1558.)

LUCIFER (above left), arriving in hell with Beelzebub, entered a new and dreadful domain, where he plotted his revenge as the adversary of humankind. Early Christian tradition, based on a passage of Isaiah and the words of Jesus – "I beheld Satan falling as lightning from heaven" – held that Satan had originated as an angel who had been thrown out of heaven because he was too proud to acknowledge the supremacy of Yahweh. (ILLUSTRATION TO MILTON'S PARADISE LOST BY JOHN MARTIN, 1827.)

THE ARCHANGEL GABRIEL (below) sits on the left hand of Yahweh and, in Hebrew literature, guards the left side of humans while they sleep. As a warrior, he will fight the last great battle with Leviathan, the symbol of chaos, at the end of time. According to Christian tradition it was Gabriel who was sent to announce the births of John the Baptist and Jesus. In Islam, he is Jibril, the angel of revelations. (ARCHANGEL GABRIEL, BYZANTINE SERBIAN ICON, 14TH CENTURY.)

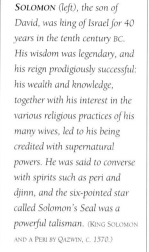

SOLOMON (left), the son of David, was king of Israel for 40 years in the tenth century BC. His wisdom was legendary, and his reign prodigiously successful: his wealth and knowledge, together with his interest in the various religious practices of his many wives, led to his being credited with supernatural powers. He was said to converse with spirits such as peri and djinn, and the six-pointed star called Solomon's Seal was a powerful talisman. (KING SOLOMON AND A PERI BY QAZWIN, C. 1570.)

THE TEMPLE (above) in Jerusalem was the outstanding achievement of Solomon's long reign. It was built using a labour force of 180,000 men, but its scale and splendour prompted the legend that Solomon's magic powers gave him command over an army of djinn who had carried out the work. When the temple was completed, it was dedicated in a ceremony lasting 14 days, during which 22,000 oxen and 120,000 sheep were sacrificed. (ILLUSTRATION FROM CALMET'S DICTIONARY OF THE HOLY BIBLE, 1732.)

MUHAMMAD (above) travelled as a young man to Syria, where he met Christians, Jews and others who believed in a single god. He became convinced that they were right. When he was about 40 he retreated to a cave on Mount Hira to wrestle with his beliefs alone. There, he was visited by the angel Jibril, who insisted that Muhammad should "recite" his beliefs, in other words, that he should preach the truth about Allah. (ILLUSTRATION FROM AN UNDATED MINIATURE.)

Z

YIMA, or Jam, or Jemshid, according to ancient Iranian mythology, was a great king. He was usually regarded as the son of *TAHMURAS*, one of the civilizing heroes, although according to some traditions the boy was born in a pillar of fire when a bolt of lightning struck the earth.

Yima governed the land wisely and justly, earning the title of the "Good Shepherd". As a priest, he was pious; as a warrior, he was strong; and as a herdsman, he was rich in cattle. He lived in a time known as the Golden Age, when death did not exist.

Because nobody died, Yima had to enlarge the earth three times, with the aid of his magic instruments. However, it came to pass that Mahrkusha, an evil demon, sent terrible floods followed by scorching summers down to earth, with the intention of annihilating all living creatures, both human beings and animals. Seeing what was about to happen, *AHURA MAZDA*, the principle of good, decided that the noble and upright Yima should be saved. He told him to build an underground dwelling place and to take into it every variety of man and beast. The fabulous chamber should also contain running water and trees, flowers and fruits. No diseased, wicked, ill-natured or deformed creature should be allowed entrance. Yima asked how he was to make this chamber, and Ahura Mazda replied that he should mould the earth with his hands and feet, as potters do. After the disaster, Yima emerged unscathed.

A later tradition claims that Yima eventually fell victim to the evil monster *AZHI DAHAKA*, who sawed him in two. It seems that he deserved this fate because he had committed the sin of pride.

ZAL, a hero of ancient Iranian mythology, was the son of Sam, a descendant of *FERIDUN*. Zal was born with white hair. Horrified by his strange appearance, his father ordered him to be left to die on the slope of a mountain. However, Simurgh, a noble vulture, rescued the baby and carried him to her nest on the peak of Mount Elburz. Simurgh was a mythical bird, said to be so old that she had seen the world destroyed three times, and had thus acquired great wisdom.

Zal grew up to become an extraordinarily beautiful young man. Sam, by now consumed with guilt for having abandoned his son, went in search of the child. He reached the home of Simurgh and entreated the vulture to return the young man to him. The bird agreed, and Sam blessed his son and called him Zal.

Zal had many adventures. On one occasion, he visited Kabul, which lay in his father's land of Hindustan. While staying with Mihrab, one of his father's servants, he learnt that his host had a beautiful daughter, Rudabeh. Without even having seen the young woman, Zal fell in love with her and she, hearing of Zal, fell in love with him. They arranged to meet in secret in a palace, which Rudabeh had filled with beautiful flowers and strewn with jewels. Rudabeh stood on a high terrace and looked down on Zal. Then, let-

ZAL was rejected as a baby by his father Sam, and exposed on a mountain. He was rescued by a fabulous bird called Simurgh, who raised him in her nest. (MINIATURE, MID 15TH CENTURY.)

ting down her beautiful hair, she told Zal to climb up it to her. Zal refused to do anything that might harm Rudabeh and instead climbed up a rope, which he managed to throw on to the terrace.

Although the young couple were deeply in love, they had to overcome the fact that Rudabeh's family were old enemies of Sam's employer, King MINUCHER. At length, Sam agreed to let Zal marry Rudabeh, particularly since astrologers had said that the couple would give birth to a great hero. That hero proved to be RUSTEM.

ZARATHUSTRA see *ZOROASTER*.

ZOHAK, according to ancient Iranian mythology, was the son of a desert king. He was persuaded by *ANGRA MAINYU*, the principle of darkness, to kill his father and seize the throne. Angra Mainyu then took up residence in Zohak's castle as his cook and persuaded the new king to introduce meat to his diet. Zohak was so pleased with his new cuisine that he promised Angra Mainyu a gift of his choosing. Angra Mainyu asked that he might kiss Zohak's shoulders, and rest his

face and eyes there. After kissing the king, Angra Mainyu disappeared. Suddenly, a snake appeared from each of Zohak's shoulders. His courtiers tried to destroy them, but each time the snakes were sliced off, they grew again.

Disguised as a doctor, Angra Mainyu returned and told Zohak that he should feed the snakes each day with human brains. In this way, Zohak himself became a demon and ruled over the world for a thousand years, during which time evil reigned supreme. Finally, one night Zohak had a terrifying dream; when

ZAL was carried by Simurgh to the highest peaks of Mount Elburz, where he grew up without his father's knowledge. Eventually, Sam was prompted by a dream to seek his son in the mountains, and the two were reconciled.

his advisers interpreted it for him, they said that it signified that he would be overthrown by a man called *FERIDUN*. Zohak ordered all children to be put to death, but the baby Feridun survived. When Feridun grew up he succeeded in killing Zohak and taking over the reins of power.

ZOROASTER, or Zarathustra, was a great religious reformer of ancient Iran. He was thought to have lived in the north-east of the country, some time in the sixth or fifth centuries BC, but scholars now believe that he lived much earlier, around 1200 BC. The compelling figure of Zoroaster gave rise to many myths. It was said that his birth was foretold from the beginning of time. The moment he was born, he burst out laughing and the whole universe rejoiced with him.

Although the evil demons, the *DRUJS*, tried to destroy the child, he was protected by *AHURA MAZDA*, the principle of good. When he reached the age of 30, Zoroaster was given numerous revelations from the *AMESA SPENTAS*, or "Holy Immortals". Once armed with these spiritual insights, Zoroaster was able to resist the temptations of *ANGRA MAINYU*, or Ahriman, the principle of darkness.

Zoroaster denounced the worship of numerous gods, which until then had been prevalent in Iran, and instead preached a purified faith, focused on the struggle between good and evil, or Ahura Mazda and Angra Mainyu. His faith was a type of monotheism, although it inclined to dualism.

It was said that on one occasion, Zoroaster visited the court of a king and performed numerous miracles, including curing the king's favourite horse, before finally winning him over to his religion. The king then waged war against numerous neighbouring kings in an attempt to convert them. According to tradition, Zoroaster was murdered at the age of 77 while at his prayers.

ZOROASTER was traditionally said to have had a miraculous birth. According to legend, his mother, Dughdova, who was a virgin, conceived after she had been visited by a shaft of light. Though evil forces repeatedly tried to destroy the baby, he was protected by Ahura Mazda. (LIEBIG "CHROMO" CARD, 19TH CENTURY.)

THE MYTHS AND LEGENDS

ZOROASTER's teaching was embraced by the Achamenian rulers of Iran, who built this square tower facing the royal rock tombs at Naqsh-i-Rustam near their capital, Persepolis. Known as the Ka'bah-i-Zardusht, it may have been used as a fire temple; fire was a Zoroastrian symbol of purity and wisdom.

It is probable that Zurvan Akarana originated as an important god of early Iranian mythology. However, in the centuries following *ZOROASTER*, devotees of the religious movement known as Zurvanism came to regard him as the primal and eternal being, beyond good and evil, who formed Ahura Mazda and Angra Mainyu in order that they should both struggle to dominate creation.

According to one tradition, Zurvan Akarana promised authority to the firstborn, leading Angra Mainyu to tear his way out of the womb. As a result, evil reigned for several thousand years. It was also said that Zurvan Akarana conceived his two offspring at the very moment when he began to doubt that he would ever give birth. In consequence, Ahura Mazda embodied his wisdom and Angra Mainyu his doubt.

ZU was the demonic tempest bird of Mesopotamian mythology who lived in the underworld and stole the tablets of fate from *ENLIL*, "Lord of the Wind". The tablets gave whoever possessed them control of the universe. The supreme god *ANU* promised sovereignty over the gods to whoever recovered the tablets. Although the fragmentary nature of the surviving text makes the outcome difficult to establish for certain, it seems that the god *MARDUK* succeeded in regaining the tablets, although in some versions of the tale Zu is overcome by *NINURTA*, Enlil's son.

ZURVAN AKARANA came to prominence in Iranian mythology as the transcendent being who gave rise to *AHURA MAZDA*, the principle of good or light, and *ANGRA MAINYU*, or Ahriman, the principle of evil or darkness.

The religious reformer *ZOROASTER* had taught that Ahura Mazda was the one true god, who was set in eternal opposition to Angra Mainyu. This dualism, which became sharper as time passed, presented a problem: if Ahura Mazda was all-powerful, then he must have created evil. The concept of Zurvan Akarana, or "Infinite Time", managed to circumvent this intellectual dilemma.

ZOROASTER was a priest, prophet and thinker who made huge innovations in religious thought. He preached a purified faith that focused on the struggle between light and darkness, or Ahura Mazda and Angra Mainyu. (SYRIAN MURAL.)

FAMILY TREES

THE BABYLONIAN PANTHEON

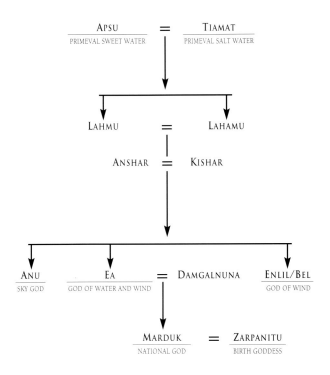

The great gods born to Anshar and Kishar disturbed the repose of their ancestors Apsu and Tiamat, who determined to destroy them. Marduk undertook to conquer Tiamat on condition that the other gods made him pre-eminent, and from her corpse he created the heavens, earth and humanity.

HORUS, the son of Isis, in battle.

THE DESCENDANTS OF RA

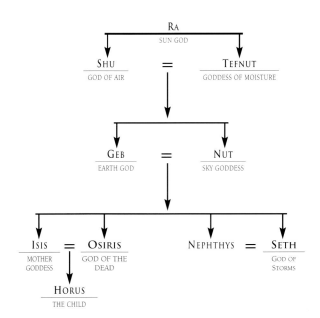

The Egyptian creator god Ra and his descendants are known collectively as the Ennead, or "Nine Gods" of Heliopolis, the site of Ra's principal sanctuary. Ra needed no consort, but spat or sneezed out Shu and Tefnut and later, from his own tears, created humanity. The children of Nut were two pairs of twins.

THE SUMERIAN PANTHEON

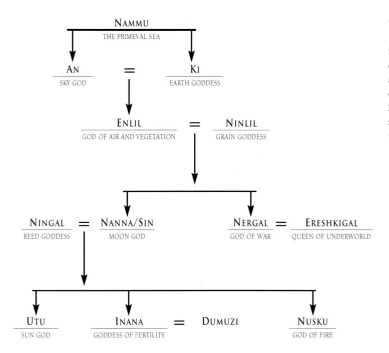

The Sumerians, living in Mesopotamia in the fourth and third millennia BC, developed a religious framework which was adapted by the Akkadians, Babylonians and other later civilizations in the region. Sumerian deities were organized into a settled pantheon by priests, who inscribed their myths on clay tablets.

NAMMU
THE PRIMEVAL SEA

AN
SKY GOD = **KI**
EARTH GODDESS

ENLIL
GOD OF AIR AND VEGETATION = **NINLIL**
GRAIN GODDESS

NINGAL
REED GODDESS = **NANNA/SIN**
MOON GOD

NERGAL
GOD OF WAR = **ERESHKIGAL**
QUEEN OF UNDERWORLD

UTU
SUN GOD

INANA
GODDESS OF FERTILITY = **DUMUZI**

NUSKU
GOD OF FIRE

THE ZOROASTRIAN HEAVENLY HIERARCHY

AHURA MAZDA/SPENTA MAINYU
THE WISE LORD

HUMANITY

In the Zoroastrian tradition, Ahura Mazda is alone worthy of worship. The seven Amesa Spentas are his creations and act as intermediaries between Ahura Mazda and his devotees. Many of the Yazatas were ancient Iranian deities who were included in the reformed religion as the servants of Ahura Mazda.

AMESA SPENTAS
SONS AND DAUGHTERS OF, OR ASPECTS OF, GOD

VOHU MANO	ASHA VAHISHA	SPENTA ARMAITI	KHSHATHRA VAIRYA	HAURVATAT	AMERETAT
GOOD THOUGHT *animals/cattle*	RIGHTEOUSNESS *fire*	DEVOTION *earth*	DOMINION *sun and heavens*	WHOLENESS *waters*	IMMORTALITY *plants*

YAZATAS
PROTECTIVE SPIRITS

ANAHITA	ATAR	HAOMA	SRAOSHA	RASHNU	MITHRA	TISHTRYA
WATER, FERTILITY	FIRE	HEALING PLANTS	OBEDIENCE, THE HEARER OF PRAYERS	JUDGMENT	TRUTH	THE DOG-STAR, SOURCE OF RAIN AND FERTILITY

HAOMA, the son of Ahura Mazda.

CHRONOLOGY

By c 4000 BC	Sumerian farming settlements in Mesopotamia.
c 3500 BC	Foundation of Sumerian city of Uruk (Erech). Technological developments of the Uruk culture include wheeled carts, sailing boats, the potter's wheel, a cuneiform writing system and the lunar calendar. Evidence of trade between the Sumerians and Egyptians has been found at Buto in the Nile Delta.
3100 BC	Unification of Egypt under the first Pharoahs. Development of heiroglyphic writing.
c 2900 BC	Evidence of trade between the Egyptians and Phoenicians.
c 2850 BC	Foundation of the Sumerian city of Ur.
c 2800-2300 BC	Old Sumerian (Early Dynastic) period.
2772 BC	Introduction of the 365-day calendar in Egypt.
2700-2180 BC	Egyptian Old Kingdom.
c 2700 BC	Construction of the pyramid of King Zoser, the first stone building in Egypt.
c 2700 BC	Reign of Gilgamesh in Uruk.
c 2600 BC	Construction of the Great Pyramid at Giza.
c 2500 BC	Egyptians conquer the Syrian coastal plain.
c 2370-2315 BC	Sargon I founds and rules the city-state of Akkad, and conquers Sumer.
c 2300-2150 BC	Akkadian period.
c 2200 BC	Foundation of the Sumerian city of Lagash.
c 2100-2000 BC	Neo-Sumerian period.
2100 BC	The Sumerian King List is compiled, recording all the kings and dynasties of Sumer.
2080-1640 BC	Egyptian Middle Kingdom.
c 2000 BC	Egyptian astronomers learn to predict the annual inundation of the Nile.
c 2000 BC	Destruction of Ur, leading to 200 years of disunity and warfare in Sumeria. Babylon becomes capital of the Mesopotamian region.

c 2000-1800 BC	Abraham leads a nomadic migration from Sumer into Canaan, then on into Egypt.
c 1900 BC	The Babylonian Epic of Gilgamesh is composed, drawing on Sumerian sources.
1900-1800 BC	The Canaanite city of Ugarit is allied with Egypt.
1792-1750 BC	Reign of Hammurabi, Amorite King of Babylon, who formulates the first comprehensive code of law.
1750-1600 BC	Egypt occupied by Hyksos from Syria, who introduce horses and chariots to the Egyptians.
16th century BC	Ugarit occupied by the Hurrians. Ugaritic cultural achievements include the earliest known alphabetical writing system.
c 1570-1085 BC	Egyptian New Kingdom.
1520-1480 BC	Egyptian expansion south and east during the reigns of Tutmosis II and III and Queen Hatshepsut.
1450-1300 BC	Hittites from Asia Minor occupy Mesopotamia, Turkey and part of Palestine.
c 1400 BC	Phoenicians settle on the Levant coast, and establish cities, including Carthage, Tyre and Sidon.
14th century BC	Ugarit is destroyed by an earthquake.

c 1367 BC	Pharoah Akhenaten proposes the first concept of a single, all-powerful deity and brings in religious reform in Egypt, reversed after his death.
1300-612 BC	Assyrians establish an empire in Mesopotamia.
13th century BC	Philistines settle on the coastal plain, thereafter called Palestine.
c 1286 BC	Egyptian expansion under Rameses the Great leads to battle against the Hittites at Qadesh and an Egyptian-Hittite treaty in 1272 BC.
c 1250 BC	Moses leads the Israelites out of Egypt.
c 1200 BC	Birth of Zoroaster.
c 1200 BC	Aramaeans take control of Damascus and Aramaic becomes the dominant language of the region.
1185 BC	Ugarit is destroyed a second time by an invasion of the "Sea People".
c 1100 BC	Assyrians colonize Syria.
c 1000 BC	David becomes king of the Hebrew tribes, now united as Israel, and makes Jerusalem his capital.
965 BC	Solomon becomes king of Israel and builds the temple in Jerusalem.
928 BC	On Solomon's death, Israel is split into two kingdoms, Israel and Judah.
c 753 BC	Foundation of Rome.
722 BC	Israel is overrun by the Assyrians, Judah survives.
705-681 BC	Reign of the Assyrian king Sennacherib. He assembles a library of Sumerian and Babylonian tablets.
671-661 BC	Assyrians invade and conquer Egypt.
664-332 BC	Late Egyptian period.
612 BC	Assyrians are expelled from Mesopotamia by the Chaldeans and Medes. Nineveh is destroyed.
612-539 BC	New Babylonian Empire.
586 BC	Jerusalem is sacked by the Babylonians. Solomon's temple is destroyed.
559-530 BC	Reign of Cyrus II, founder of the Persian empire.
558-330 BC	Achaemenids (Medes and Persians) rule Iran.
539 BC	Babylon is invaded and conquered by Cyrus II.
525 BC	Persians occupy Egypt, and the Persian empire extends from the Indus River to the Aegean.
336 BC	Philip of Macedon unites the Greek city states.
331 BC	Philip's son, Alexander the Great, begins his conquest of the Persian empire, reaching India in 326 BC.
211 BC	Defeat of Carthage gives Rome control of Western Mediterranean, and it invades Greece.
204 BC	The Black Stone of Cybele is brought from Phrygia to Rome.
192-189 BC	War between the Greek Seleucids and Rome.
168 BC	Jewish revolt against the Seleucid King Antiochus Epiphanes, leads to the foundation of the Jewish Maccabean kingdom.
146 BC	Carthage is destroyed. North Africa, Egypt, Asia Minor and Greece are all ruled by Rome.
40 BC	Herod the Great is appointed king of Judea.
29 BC-AD 14	Reign of Augustus Caesar.
1st century AD	Christianity arrives in Egypt.
70	Following a Jewish rebellion against Rome, Jerusalem is destroyed by Emperor Titus.
135	A final Jewish revolt is put down by Emperor Hadrian and the Jews are scattered.
3rd century	The beginning of the rise of Christianity in the Roman empire.
212	All inhabitants of the Roman empire are granted citizenship.
226-652	Sassanians rule Iran, overthrowing the Parthians.
306-337	Reign of the Roman Emperor Constantine, who is converted to Christianity in 312.
c 310	Romans end the persecution of Christians.

330	Foundation of Constantinople, which becomes capital of the eastern Roman empire.
395	Division of the Roman empire into Western and Eastern (Byzantine) halves.
476	End of the Roman empire.
534-628	Persian invasions of Syria.
570/1	Birth of Muhammad in Mecca.
610/1	Muhammad experiences divine revelation and begins his ministry; Islam spreads through Asia.
616	Persians conquer Egypt and Asia Minor, and besiege Constantinople.
622	Muhammad is forced to leave Mecca and goes to Medina. This date is later adopted as the first year of the Muslim calendar.
630	Muhammad conquers Mecca at the head of an army from Medina, and stamps out idolatry.
632	Death of Muhammad.
656	Beginning of the Islamic split between Sunnis and Shi'ites. Damascus becomes the capital of the Arab empire.

c 660	Arabs drive Persians out of Mesopotamia, and occupy Syria and Egypt.
711-720	Arabs advance across Spain, occupying it and part of France.
750	Baghdad becomes the centre of Arab power, at the beginning of the Golden Age of Islam.
867	Turks seize power in Egypt and Syria. The Arabs lose control of the Mediterranean.
10th century	The Iranian epic poem, the Shah-Nameh, is composed, recording the exploits of the hero Rustem.
10th century	The Turks are converted to Islam.
969	Egypt is invaded by Shi'ite Fatimid Arabs, who establish Cairo as their capital, rivalling the caliphate of Baghdad. Cairo becomes a major trade centre.
1050	Capture of Baghdad by Turkish Seljuks.
1071	Seljuks take Syria and Palestine, occupy Asia Minor and threaten Byzantium.
1096-7	First Crusade.
1100	Christians capture Jerusalem and set up crusader kingdoms.
1187	Jerusalem is recaptured by Saladin.
1220	Genghis Khan seizes Persia.
1453-1548	Ottoman invasions of Constantinople, Cairo, Vienna and Persia.
1571	Battle of Lepanto ends Ottoman dominance in the Mediterranean.
1799	Discovery of the Rosetta Stone by Napoleonic troops leads to the decipherment of Egyptian heiroglyphs by Jean-François Champollion, 1822.
1916	Ottoman empire is overthrown.
1922	Discovery of the tomb of Tutankhamen.
1929	Discovery of the remains of Ugarit, Syria.
1947-56	Discovery of the Dead Sea Scrolls.

INDEX

Picture Acknowledgements
The Publishers are grateful to the agencies listed below for kind permission to reproduce the following images in this book.

AKG, London: p61 National Museum, Cairo; p6 Kunsthistorisches Museum, Vienna; p7 Haifa University; p12br Musee du Louvre, Paris; p14t National Museum, Damascus; p19tr Kunsthistorisches Museum, Vienna; p19bl Musee du Louvre, Paris; p21tl National Museum, Cairo; p22 Museo Naxionale Romano delle Terme, Rome; p23br Musee du Louvre, Paris; p25tr Museo Ostiense, Ostia; p26tr Hosios Loukas Monastery, Greece; p28bl Museo Capitular de la Catedral, Gerona; p29tr Neuburg Monastery, Austria; p30tl Nationalmuseum, Aleppo; p31r Galleria degli Uffizi, Florence; p33 Icon Gallery, Sveti Kliment; p37; p47tr Kunsthistorisches Museum, Vienna; p49b Musee du Louvre, Paris; p53 British Museum, London; p55 Bibliotheque Municipale, Dijon; p56; p58b Aegyptishes Museum, Berlin; p59 Kunsthistorisches Museum, Vienna; p60tl Musee du Louvre, Paris; p62 Egyptian Museum, Cairo; p63t; p65tr Musee du Louvre, Paris; p65bl Musee du Louvre; p65br Museo Nazionale Romano delle Terme, Rome; p66 Haifa University; p70 Mossul Museum; p73 Royal Collection, Copenhagen; p77 National Museum, Cairo; p83tl Serbian Monastery of Hilandar; p87b Yale University Art Gallery, New Haven.

Ancient Art and Architecture: p12bl; p14b; p15tl; p16b; p25tl; p27bl; p30br; p34; p36tl; p40tr; p40bl; p43; p44bl; p45b; p49tr; p50tl; p50b; p52b; p57bl; p68t; p68b; p71b; p76t; p80.

Ancient Egypt Picture Library: p19mr; p21br; p24bl; p32b; p36tr; p36bl; p39mr; p44bl; p49tl; p52tr; p58t; p63b.

Bridgeman Art Library: p13tl Museo Diocesano de Solsona, Lerida; p20 Lauros-Giraudon; p24tl Fitzwilliam Museum, Cambridge; p31 private collection; p32t Beatty Library, Chester; p41bl Giraudon.

Christie's Art Gallery: p24br; p39tr; p39br; p75bl; p75br; p82tl & br; p83tr; p84.

Corbis: p13br Mimmo Jodice; p15br Gianni Dagli Orti; p29tl Bettmann; p46t Charles & Josette Lenars; p64t The State Russian Museum; p78 Nik Wheeler; p80 Paul Almasy; p81r Gianne Dagli Orti; p82tr Michael Nicholson; p83bl Bettman; p85; p87 Paul Almasy.

CM Dixon: p16t; p19ml; p35; p54b.

Edimedia: p15lt.

ET Archive: p2; p8bl; p17br; p18t Musee du Louvre, Paris; p18b Egyptian Museum, Cairo; p19tl Archeological Museum, Cairo; p35; p39mr; p42tr Musee du Louvre, Paris; p44tr Hittite Museum, Ankara; p48 Christie's; p51 San Vitale Ravenna, Italy; p69l Musee du Louvre; p86.

Mary Evans: p10/11 and p57t; p29br; p38t; p38b; p39tl; p39bl; p45t; p46b; p47bl; p47bm; p72b; p74b; p75tr; p75tl; p79b; p82bl; p83mr.

Michael Holford: p17tr; p67t; p71t; p74tr; p74ml.

Panos Pictures: p64b Jean-Léo Dugast.